What others are saying about this book:

Spring, summer, fall or winter, you'll find everything you need in *"The Veggie Queen™: Vegetables Get the Royal Treatment"* to transform the season's finest produce into delicious recipes.
Holly Rudin-Braschi, MA, ACSM, author "Grill Power" (Beyond Words Publishing)

Jill Nussinow has truly given vegetables the royal treatment they so richly deserve. Here veggies shine with imagination and creativity, with seasonality and seasoning. Simply delicious and healthy dishes like Asparagus with Black Bean Sauce for spring, Roasted Red Pepper and Tomato Soup for summer, Stuffed Swiss Chard for fall, and Layered Polenta Casserole for winter are sure to satisfy.
Aliza Green, author of Field Guide to Produce

"I like Jill's recipes. Fresh, simple ideas. Mostly quick and easy. This is a book to keep handy in your kitchen."
Marie Simmons, cookbook author, Fig Heaven

Jill has compiled her best recipes into *The Veggie Queen* for your benefit. Her love of vegetables and mastery of their preparation and cooking comes through on every page. Making these recipes will not only provide gustatory pleasure, but immense health benefits.
David Pressman, Patent Lawyer, San Francisco, Author of Patent It Yourself (Nolo Press), World's Best Selling Patent Guide

The Veggie Queen – a timely cookbook with a fresh approach to seasonal eating with exciting recipes that are delicious as well as health promoting.
Dixie Mahy, President, San Francisco Vegetarian Society.

"Jill knows more about vegetables than any other chef or dietitian we've met. She understands their nutritional importance and shows readers how to turn vegetables into unique dishes, creating enjoyment for everyone."
John and Mary McDougall – the McDougall Live-in Program, Santa Rosa, California

Vegetables are so dear to me that I consider myself a closet vegetarian. Jill Nussinow's recipes are so beautifully balanced - combining salty, savory, earthy, and sweet - that I'm considering upgrading my status to honorary. The Veggie Queen™'s benevolent approach to her subjects ensures they fulfill their delicious potential – I will be cooking my way through the seasons with this book. *Carrie Brown, Proprietor JImtown Store and author of The Jimtown Store Cookbook, Recipes from Sonoma County's Favorite Country Market, Harper Collins Publishers 2002*

The Veggie Queen™

The Veggie Queen™

Vegetables Get the Royal Treatment

More than 100 seasonal vegetable recipes

Jill Nussinow, M.S, R.D.

Foreword by Ellen Ecker Ogden
Illustrations by Josef Sorensen

Vegetarian Connection Press, Santa Rosa, California

The Veggie Queen™
Vegetables Get the Royal Treatment
By Jill Nussinow, M.S, R.D.

Cover Illustration by Michel Stong, © 2005
Illustrations by Josef Sorensen, © 2005
Book and cover design: Tony Monaco
Edited by Laurie Reaume
Back cover photo: Ed Aiona

FIRST EDITION
ISBN: 978-0-9767085-0-6
Library of Congress Control Number: 2005925045

Published by Vegetarian Connection Press, Santa Rosa, California
PO Box 6042, Santa Rosa, CA 95406-0042
www.vegetarianconnection.com

Printed in Canada

*To Mother Earth and my parents, Mickey and Bernie Nussinow,
who have inspired and encouraged me to do what I love.*

Acknowledgements

I couldn't have completed this project without help. Big thank yous go to:

My husband, Rick Cratty, for tasting almost everything that I've made except dishes that contain mushrooms or tempeh. Without his support very little would be possible.

My son Shane, who despite being quite particular (a nice word for picky) has tried lots of different recipes and vegetables. He has shown me that children will eat a variety of foods when they're offered and available. How many kid's favorites include tofu, pineapple guava, cucumbers and tomatoes?

My parents, Mickey and Bernie Nussinow, and sisters, Andrea Nussinow and Donna Lampert, for always being there for me; for not making me think that I was strange when I chose to become a vegetarian, and then for adopting vegetarian ways too (when they were ready).

Michel Stong who said that she would draw the Veggie Queen. She's created a vision so beautiful it almost makes me want to cry. I applaud your talent and generosity.

Josef Sorenson, the 15-year old who willingly agreed to illustrate this book. And the Mushroom Goddesses for making our friendship possible. Great job Joe.

Laurie Reaume, my friend, fellow vegetarian and book editor, for using her word whacker to trim and shape my words. And for encouraging me along the way with her wry and punny humor.

Christine Piccin, colleague and friend, for whipping my words into shape and sharing her extensive food knowledge.

Ellen Horstman for her assistance at my classes and continually making me look great without taking credit for all that she does. Without her organization, neatness and attention to detail my pots and pans would never shine.

Ellen Ecker Ogden for writing the foreword. She's somebody special who shares my love for vegetables. I wish that I had her green thumb and gardening talent.

Beth (Elizabeth) Snow who updates my website and much more than that. I only wish that she could help me everyday.

Holly Rudin-Braschi for being one of the best cheerleaders that one could ever have.

Clare Venet, my yoga teacher, for providing a nurturing space for me to practice. Without her I am sure that I would not have had the strength, flexibility and presence of heart and mind to carry on upright every day.

Barbara Stone, my longest time friend who is always there on the other end of the computer, listening to the sordid details of everything. And although they aren't vegetarian, for sending clam vibes.

Bob Nemerovski of Ramekins Cooking School for pushing me to teach Vegetable Workshop (instead of vegetarian) classes thus turning me into the Veggie Queen.

Farmers – those who I know personally, and living elsewhere – for whom I have the utmost respect and gratitude that you steward the land, nourishing it and us simultaneously. Your vegetables provide my inspiration.

All of my students at Santa Rosa Junior College, the McDougall programs, and elsewhere who have taught me almost as much as I have taught them. There is nothing like being in a kitchen with more than 20 students and seeing what "really" happens.

My other food professional colleagues and friends, too numerous to name, who have provided encouragement, as well as sharing their trials and tribulations. Thanks are not quite enough.

I truly thank everyone who has helped me get where I am today. And there are lots of you. From the, top, sides and bottom of my heart…

Table of Contents

The Veggie Queen's Morsels and Tidbits

Preface

We often think about parents, mothers especially, reminding their children to eat their veggies. Well, my mom never had to do that with me. The summer when I was four, I was helping my mother shell peas to add to macaroni salad. I am not sure how many peas actually made it into the salad, as I remember eating lots of them.

Also when I was four, my mother discovered that I liked eating red peppers. She had a garden. So, we went to the garden store and bought a pepper plant. I tasted a pepper when it had grown and turned bright red. Instead of being sweet, the pepper was very hot and most unpleasant. It was too much for my immature digestive system. Yet, I still love to eat sweet red peppers and will even eat mildly hot ones.

Before I was born my maternal grandfather suffered a serious heart attack while still in his 40s. My grandparents went to Duke University where Dr. Kempner prescribed a diet. Today it's called "the rice diet". My grandmother helped my grandfather faithfully follow the diet. When they came to our house for dinner, she brought his food in containers tucked into a plaid Thermos™ bag. The fare almost always was Minute Rice™ (thus the rice diet moniker), a potato to bake, Nanna's tomato sauce, a chicken breast or piece of fish and usually another vegetable. I would always want to sit next to Poppa and eat some of his potato, tomato sauce and other vegetable, shunning the slab of meat on my plate.

Vegetables have beckoned me for a long time. In 1988, when I moved from Los Angeles to Sonoma County I wanted to do three things: 1) join the Sonoma County Farmlands group to help protect existing farm land, 2) join and support the California Certified Organic Farmers, and 3) write about food from field to table. I did all three almost immediately. A big accomplishment was seeing the Sonoma County Bounty column that I wrote for the Farmlands Group appear in local newspapers. I met many of the county's farmers and learned who grew what and who grew the best. I visited local farms and still do. Since then my connection to my food has only grown stronger.

Some people head to church on Sunday mornings. I jump in the car and drive to the farmer's market. I believe that I am seeking something similar to what one might find at church. I get a connection, spiritual fulfillment, an opportunity to thank the people who produce the food that I eat, the chance to speak with people outside my usual circle and more. The farmer's market is not just about buying fruits, vegetables and other farm fresh products. It is about community, knowing where I belong and how I fit in.

One morning, a stranger and I commented about the "imperfect" peaches and how it was only their looks that made them less desirable, but what was wrong with that? We agreed that taste is the most important quality.

One farmer sells "ugly" tomatoes. They may have a spot or a bruise, or even a scar. They are definitely not perfect, but what is? Acceptance is most important.

I met Debra at the farmer's market the other day wearing a red beret. I had almost worn mine that morning. Until that day I had never spoken to Debra. I felt compelled to learn her name. We agreed that we'd seen each other there a "million" times. That day we kept bumping into one another over persimmons, apples, greens and broccoli. I now feel like I know a fellow traveler, not a stranger, on my path to wholesome produce.

I love what I do and feel passionate about passing on my love of vegetables and plant foods to you. I hope that you can share my sense of excitement at picking the first tomato of the season, finding a chanterelle mushroom deep in the woods or munching on the crunchiest, juiciest Painted Serpent cucumber.

I am awed and inspired by nature. I love watching things grow and consider plant foods the ultimate gift that our Mother Earth has to offer. I want to elevate and glorify vegetables, giving them a renewed importance in your life and on your plate.

Foreword

Talking about food at the table is fairly safe, unless you are sitting down to dinner with a vegetarian. Then you may learn more about food than you really want to know. Food takes on a whole new language.

In addition to vegetarians' health consciousness, there's a strong moral fiber to their philosophy of eating. They express concern for the animals. They are concerned about the environment and how a meat-based diet depletes natural resources compared to one based on vegetable products. Land is over-grazed; grain is squandered on feeding livestock instead of people. And with our current agricultural system, chemicals invade the soils as well as the animals, which may return to haunt us through cancer and other illnesses.

Yet vegetarians also love good, wholesome food that reflects their personal values and honors the health of the earth, as well as their own bodies. Jill Nussinow, a.k.a. The Veggie Queen™ is well versed in all aspects of vegetable cuisine. In this book, she combines her sincere love of the vegetable world with wit, humor, and of course inspiring recipes.

The Veggie Queen™ reigns over the vegetable kingdom by sharing her best recipes from twenty years of teaching, writing and cooking for family and friends. Her collection of recipes and reflections are a reminder that talking about food goes beyond simple cooking instructions, into the realm of food that sings with color and charms the palate with a vibrant blend of flavors.

Vegetarians may surrender some traditional pleasures of the table, but they don't miss out on all of the fun. In fact, they eat better than most, especially if they love to cook. Good food is a celebration of life, and vegetarian cuisine honors and respects the fruits (and vegetables) of the earth. Through a vocabulary rich in terroir or connection to place, Jill Nussinow shares her joy for the vegetarian lifestyle.

- Ellen Ecker Ogden

Co-founder The Cook's Garden catalog
and author of From the Cook's Garden cookbook

Introduction

In 1993, shortly after my son Shane was born, I wrote a book, *Vegetarian Cooking for Everyone, Volume 1*. I called it a cookbooklet. It had 44 recipes and almost as many typos. I was compelled to get that small book into the world. I had plans to write volume 2 but didn't realize how much of my energy would go into being a parent. Also, Deborah Madison's book *Vegetarian Cooking for Everyone* (I knew that I had a great title) was distributed by a big-name publisher. So I put my writing plans on hold.

I've talked about writing this book for years. My cooking class students have continually asked for it. And with Shane approaching his teenage years, it seemed like I was ready to go through the birthing process again but this time as The Veggie Queen™.

This is not a comprehensive cookbook, or a tome about vegetables. It's not necessary to read this from cover to cover but you might miss something that I have to share. It's the cookbook that I kept wishing that I had on my bookshelf; one with recipes laid out according to the seasons, using almost exclusively seasonal ingredients. Therefore, you will not find recipes for fresh tomatoes, eggplant or zucchini in winter. Those will be found either in the summer or fall chapters. Of course there is some seasonal variation according to your climate and geography. If you have great homegrown or local tomatoes in January, look in the index so you can find recipes that use them.

And if a recipe does call for tomatoes in the winter such as in Black Bean Chili, use the best canned tomatoes that you can find. You can always substitute high quality canned or frozen products to save time. We all have busy lives and eating good food is what matters most. Don't feel badly about opening a can if you must.

In addition to using seasonal ingredients, I emphasize buying local, sustainably and organically grown produce because I think that it's fresher and tastier. Although the purchase price may be higher, the cost is justified in the long run. Just-picked produce doesn't usually have to travel long distances and holds up better. My farmer's market salad blend easily lasts a week. When I buy bagged salad mix, it usually gets slimy just a few days after I open the bag. There is also a lower environmental cost as sustainable and organic practices nurture the soil which I am hoping increases nutritive value. (The studies are not conclusive at this point.) And there's less fossil fuel used for transport. I consider this a win-win situation.

Nutritionally, the bottom line is that eating vegetables is only healthy if they make it to your mouth. If emptying part of the contents from a bag of frozen vegetables into a bowl and popping it into the microwave is your style, that's fine. It doesn't do any good to have fresh vegetables turn into science experiments in the refrigerator. Fresh only stays fresh so long. I suggest using bagged salad mix and precut veggies if that's what gets you to eat them. And that's what this book is all about – eating more vegetables.

Scattered among the recipes are sidebars that contain information about various vegetables, cooking techniques, farmers and more. It's where I get to share more than just a recipe. You can learn about the faces associated with the food that I buy and my vegetable experiences. In each chapter you will find a range of recipes that go in order from appetizers, salads, soups, side dishes, main courses and dessert. What you won't find are recipes that include green peppers (since they are unripe and my body somehow knows that) or fennel. If you like these, feel free to add them to any recipe, as long as they are in season.

In addition to the four seasonal chapters, I have included an Anytime chapter that includes recipes that can be used year round or that are easily adapted to seasonal produce. My final chapter is Pressure Cooking. Using a pressure cooker has changed the way that I cook. Great meals seem to appear in almost no time.

Although this is not a quick, easy or nutrition-based cookbook, you will find all of that here. These recipes contain many different, and possibly new-to-you, vegetables. I encourage you to aim for variety and to taste, cook and eat new vegetables. Shoot for five servings a day or more. I wish you luck on your journey into the vegetable kingdom. Thanks for letting me come along.

Jill Nussinow a.k.a. The Veggie Queen™

Note for McDougallers

For those of you who know about the McDougall program developed by John McDougall, M.D., please feel free to skip this paragraph and move on to the next one. Dr. McDougall developed a no-added oil, vegan (no animal product) diet for people to follow to improve their health and well being. I teach that program in Santa Rosa throughout the year. People from all across the United States and foreign countries attend the 10-day programs or weekend sessions. I am honored that I get to teach the cooking segment. Since I teach classes beyond the McDougall program, some of my recipes use ingredients such as oil that are not on the diet. Therefore, I have written this note. If you want more information on Dr. McDougall's diet or the program please go online to www.drmcdougall.com.

If you follow the McDougall program most of my recipes will adapt easily to your diet. Some of them will not. The biggest recipe modification involves simply eliminating the oil used for sautéing the initial recipe ingredients. Cross off the oil and then do what I call "dry sauté".

Dry sautéing is a technique that requires a good nonstick pot or pan. Put the pan over medium heat for a few minutes. Then add the ingredients in the order listed. The key is to watch to be sure that nothing is sticking or burning. If that begins to happen, add water, broth, juice or wine, a tablespoon at a time to release the food. Do not add so much that the ingredients get soggy. They will then be steaming, not sautéing. I have found that this is the best method for extracting the most flavors from food.

Many people object to salad dressing sliding off their salad. When making salad dressings, instead of using oil you can use Oil Substitute for Salad Dressing (found in the Anytime chapter, p. 99), or 1/8th to 1/2 teaspoon of guar or xanthan gum. Either of these gums will thicken your dressings without adding any flavor. As an added benefit they may also help lower your cholesterol. This is the easiest way to achieve the texture that oil produces. I hope that you will find my salad dressings quite flavorful.

Some of my recipes contain soy cheese. You may choose to leave it out, or not. Often the cheese adds salt to the recipe. If you'd like to replicate that flavor you can try adding capers, chopped kalamata or green olives or another salty ingredient. When cheese is a garnish, it is easily omitted. Instead, add a dash or sprinkle of salt on top of your food.

If a recipe calls for lite coconut milk, omit it or use a bit of soy or other nondairy milk and a touch of coconut extract. It will provide a similar flavor without all the fat (most of which is saturated).

My recipes include some nuts and seeds as garnishes. Occasionally I use tahini or other nut butter. If you are avoiding any "rich" foods while following the McDougall diet you can adapt these recipes by leaving out "rich" ingredients or skip those recipes entirely. You will still find plenty of recipes in this book that will work for you.

I have included notes for you throughout the book so that you can determine the recipes that need to be adapted to your way of eating, and provide the instruction for you to do that. If any ingredients seem questionable to you, then I suggest that you omit them. These recipes were written for the general public and occasionally a revision will result in an unacceptable finished product. I hope that this doesn't happen for you. If it does, please feel free to contact me and share your experience. There is always something to learn.

I consider eating a large salad every day an easy recipe for weight loss and maintenance. You'll find many salad recipes. You'll find easy ways to eat many servings of vegetables daily.

My hope is that you'll eat healthfully and live a long happy life. Thank you for letting me be a part of it and please attribute some of your health to the vegetables.

Kitchen Equipment – Essentials and Beyond

This list contains what I consider kitchen essentials -- beyond your hands, knives, pot and pans. When preparing meals, consider items that might make your cooking life easier. You might not want or need all of them.

Citrus squeezer – an enameled metal device into which you put a half lime, lemon or orange with the cut side down. It has rounded cup with wholes in the bottom, two handles and when you pull the one down over the other, it squeezes out the juice. I can use my lemon type for limes, lemons, small oranges and even pieces of grapefruit. Available at most kitchen stores or www.melissaguerra.com.

Fine mesh strainer – necessary for rinsing quinoa. And since quinoa is my favorite whole grain, I've got to have one. Get one that's about 6 inches across so that it's large enough to use for straining stock, too.

Garlic roller – a simple rubber-like tube into which you insert a clove of garlic and then roll. This action removes the outer peel of the clove. It works best for older garlic, as the peel on more freshly harvested garlic does not like to release its paper skin. You can always use the blade of your chef's knife and give the garlic a good whack.

Hand, stick or immersion blender – it is invaluable for blending soups. It is far safer and easier than using a blender or food processor, as you avoid transferring hot liquid. Put the immersion blender right into the hot pot. Just remember not to lift it out when it's going, or you and your kitchen will be splattered. I have a Cuisinart model that has an extendible shaft and comes with a small food processor attachment. It eliminates the need for a 2-cup processor (see below).

Heat resistant spatula or spoonula – have at least one or two of these around as they do not scratch your nonstick cookware and can be in heat up to 500 degrees F. without melting. In fact, why not get rid of the spatulas that can melt?

Kitchen scissors – use for chopping herbs, cutting pieces long pasta and more. Reserve them only for kitchen use; buy another pair for your plants.

Large food processor – comes with a steel blade, slicing disk and grating disk. Get one that holds at least 7 cups. If I could have two food processors on hand, I'd get a 2-cup and an 11-cup, or larger, model. A processor can save you lots of time in the kitchen. Put it on the countertop so that you will use it all the time. Be careful when storing and using the blades. They are extremely sharp.

Microplane™ grater – this is the kitchen version of the tool found in a woodworking shop. It's a sharp, multi-purpose tool that works well for grating ginger, garlic, citrus zest and chocolate among other food items.

OXO™ Look-into measuring cup – I don't know who thought up this ingenious idea. It comes in sizes from one-quarter of a cup to four cups. Using this eliminates bending over to see if you have the correct liquid measurement. You just look down into the plastic cup and can see the measurement gradations.

Small food processor – this is great for chopping small amounts of garlic and onions, and for making salad dressings. A 2- or 3-cup model is perfect.

Spice (coffee) grinder – Get one that you dedicate only for spices, herbs, nuts and seeds so your spices don't taste like coffee, or vice versa. The flavor of freshly ground, toasted spices cannot be replicated from a jar of spice. If you don't have one you can use a blender but not the new type with a wide bottom. It's got to be an older model. The food processor will NOT work for this. (Trust me, I've tried it.) My Grind Central™ from Cuisinart is wonderful because the grinding mechanism was designed for easy removal and cleaning.

Tongs – keep a pair of metal tongs around for tossing greens when they are sautéing, or removing roasted peppers from the grill. For outdoor use, be sure that they have long enough handles. For salads, I have a great pair of wooden serving tongs (seen in my DVD, Creative Low-fat Vegan Cuisine) made by Mac Davis in Grass Valley, California. Contact him at (530) 888-7857 and tell him Jill sent you.

Whisk – a teeny, tiny one is essential for mixing up small amounts of salad dressings, especially if you are stirring in guar or xanthan gum, or for mixing arrowroot and water. Be sure to use a coated, heat-resistant whisk when making gravy in your nonstick pan.

The discovery of a new dish does more for human happiness
than the discovery of a new star.

Anthelme Brillat-Savarin
The Physiology of Taste, 1825
French gourmet & lawyer (1755 - 1826)

Spring

Spring is rebirth, end of winter, beginning of the thaw. Bulbs bloom, birds return and the foods we eat are lighter. Salads seem more appealing now than they did in winter. The prospect of shedding our clothes, and perhaps a few extra pounds, becomes real as summer beckons.

No matter where you live, whether spring arrives in March or May, it has the ability to lift your spirits and change your mood. The days of roots and tubers of winter are behind us. Vegetables peek out from the ground. Shoots of asparagus appear. Artichokes form their flowers, which we eat. Garlic sends its greens out to scout for sun. Onions get plucked from the earth before they form a papery skin. And if we are lucky, we get to eat them all. Perhaps the peas arrive. And it's time to make my favorite spring risotto with peas, green garlic, asparagus and saffron. Getting outdoors helps us connect with the natural world and remember our place in it. Creativity abounds. Inspiration strikes. Time to get cooking.

Orange and Onion Salad on Greens

Serves 4 to 6

*E*ither spinach or baby greens provide a dashing and tasty backdrop for the onions and oranges. This recipe may seem unusual but the flavors all complement one another. McDougallers can omit the oil or add just a pinch of guar or xanthan gum to the dressing ingredients to thicken them a bit.

3	**cups spinach or mixed baby greens, such as mustard, arugula, dandelion**
3	**large navel oranges**
1/2	**medium red onion, thinly sliced into rings**
	Rice wine vinegar
1	**teaspoon orange zest**
2	**tablespoons orange juice**
2	**tablespoons rice wine vinegar**
2	**teaspoons olive oil**
2	**tablespoons garlic or regular chives, minced or green onions**
1/2	**teaspoon salt**
	Pinch of cayenne
	Black pepper, to taste

Wash greens and dry them in a spinner. Wrap loosely in a damp towel and refrigerate.

Zest oranges. Then remove sections from oranges by cutting off the ends. Slice down the sides of the oranges, removing the peel and underlying white pith. With the orange flesh exposed, run the knife inside the membrane on each side of the section. Remove section and put in a non-reactive bowl like glass or stainless steel. Alternatively, you may remove the ends of the oranges and cut the orange crosswise into whole sections.

Toss the onion with the rice vinegar to draw out its pink color. Set aside.

Combine ingredients orange zest through black pepper to make the dressing.

Put greens in the bottom of a large bowl. Remove onions from vinegar. Toss the oranges with the dressing. Arrange the oranges and onions on top of greens.

Oriental Cucumber Salad

Serves 4 -6

*T*his is an easy to make fat-free salad that is great for the late spring and all summer, as it does not have to be refrigerated to taste good. Because I can get them, I usually use a combination of Armenian, regular and lemon cucumbers. Use what you can get, English cucumbers work well. Cucumbers are usually one of the first vegetables, after radishes, to show up at the spring farmer's markets.

3 medium or 6 small cucumbers,
use some lemon cucumbers for color variety
1/2 large onion, sliced thinly
1 cup of rice wine vinegar
3 Tablespoons sesame seeds, toasted

Thinly slice cucumbers. Don't peel unless skin is bitter. Put into glass or ceramic bowl. Add onion. Add vinegar. Cover bowl. Stir at least once in 24 hours. Marinate at least 1 day. Just before serving mix in sesame seeds.

Note: If you like you can add fresh dill to this recipe. This low calorie dish will last up to four days in the refrigerator.

Neat Neil

When Neil Dunaetz finished farming for the season in 2004 I sensed that it might have been his final season. Abby, his girlfriend and partner, does not like the farming business. Neil mentioned a number of times that he had thought about quitting. If so, his departure will be a big loss to the local farmer's market.

Neil first showed up at the Sebastopol, California farmer's market 4 years ago. I am always a bit skeptical of a new vendor at the market. So the first time that I saw Neil, slim, bespectacled with pristine, handwritten signs and a feather duster to keep his produce clean, I only bought a couple of cucumbers. I had my "regular people" who supplied me with cucumbers, squash and more. I didn't have a big need to buy from Neil. My shopping habits would have to change and I am a creature of habit. It would be hard. But after tasting the cucumber I bought from Neil that first week, I went back for more. Somehow Neil's care for the soil came through in his produce.

I became a fan of Neil's Easysweet Farm, even taking my junior college and other classes for tours of his farm. They got to see his neatly planted fields, his packing shed with neatly stacked boxes and his home next door. Neil lived in a blue tent, next to the land which he farmed.

When the first winter came, Neil, a native of Michigan, thought that he wanted to live outdoors. While we were discussing this at the market a customer overheard the conversation and offered him a trailer on her property. Neil was reluctant. Since it can be quite stormy here, I prodded him to write down the woman's number. "Give that woman a call," I said as I was leaving. And he did. He spent the winter indoors. But come spring Neil moved back out to his tent.

Now he lives comfortably in a house with Abby. Hopefully in the spring he will recall his love of the outdoors and will be anxious to get his hands in the soil and grow something for all of us to enjoy. I hope that when I next see Neil, he'll be at his farmer's market stand offering offbeat crops like West Indies Gherkins or standards such as Japanese or lemon cucumbers, all neatly displayed and properly dusted. If he's not there I will surely miss him.

Thai Rice, Snow Pea and Mushroom Salad

Serves 4 to

*T*he flavors of Thai cooking are so enticing. Here they are combined to make an incredibly tasty salad. It is definitely rich since it uses coconut milk. I almost always use lite coconut milk since it adds the flavor with less fat.

McDougallers must adjust this recipe. Omit the coconut milk and use 2 1/4 cups water to cook the rice. After it's cooked, stir in coconut extract for flavor. For the dressing use nondairy milk, a pinch of guar or xanthan gum and coconut extract instead of coconut milk. Be sure to use all the seasonings, they are essential.

1 1/2	cups raw jasmine rice, rinsed
2	fresh lemongrass stalks, cut into 3 or 4 pieces
1/2-1	fresh chile, seeded and minced
1	teaspoon canola or other vegetable oil
1 1/2	cups boiling water
3/4	cup lite or regular coconut milk
1/2	teaspoon salt

1	medium red or orange pepper
1/2	pound snow peas, stemmed and cut in half diagonally
12	ounces assorted mushrooms, shiitake, crimini, oyster or white
2	teaspoons minced garlic
2	teaspoons grated fresh ginger root
1	finely chopped kaffir lime leaf
1/2	fresh chile, minced (seeded if you want it milder)
2	teaspoons canola or other vegetable oil

Dash of salt
Chopped fresh basil
Roasted peanuts

Dressing:

1/4	cup lite or regular coconut milk
3	tablespoons fresh lime juice
1	teaspoon sugar
1/2	teaspoon salt
2	tablespoons chopped fresh basil, preferably Thai basil
2	tablespoons chopped fresh cilantro or mint

In a small heavy pot with a tight fitting lid, sauté the rice, lemongrass and chile in the oil for 1 to 2 minutes, stirring constantly. Add the boiling water, coconut milk and salt and bring to a boil; then stir, reduce the heat to very low, cover and cook until all of the liquid has been absorbed, about 15 minutes.

Meanwhile, whisk together all of the dressing ingredients in a small bowl and set aside. Seed the pepper and cut into thin strips about 1 1/2 inches long. Blanch the pepper strips in boiling water for 1 to 2 minutes, until just tender, and set aside in a serving bowl. Blanch the snow peas in boiling water until just tender, about 1 minute and add to the serving bowl.

When the rice is tender, remove the lemongrass pieces, fluff the rice with a fork and set it aside to cool.

Remove and discard any tough stems from the mushrooms, then rinse and slice the caps into bite size pieces. In a skillet, combine the garlic, ginger root, kaffir lime, chile and oil and sauté on medium heat for 1 minute, stirring constantly. Add the mushrooms and salt and toss well. Cover the skillet, reduce the heat, and cook until the mushrooms are softened and begin to release their juices, 3 to 5 minutes.

Add the sautéed mushrooms and cooled rice to the serving bowl, pour on the dressing and toss well. Serve at room temperature, garnished with basil and peanuts.

Mushrooms in My Bathtub

I saw a former junior college student of mine this morning and told her that I am growing oyster mushrooms in my bathtub. "Are you going to write about it?" Noriko asked.

"I don't think so," I replied, wondering what you might think about this practice. Am I such a lousy housekeeper that I can actually grow fungi in the tub? No. I went to SOMA (Sonoma County Mycological Association at www.somamushrooms.org) Mushroom Camp a few weeks ago and we made oyster mushroom bags specifically intended for growing mushrooms. (You may have a local mycological or mushrooming group.)

I did it last year, too, but with less success. Last year I didn't receive the instructions for how to take care of my plastic bag of sterilized straw laced with mushroom spawn. Somehow I thought that the mushrooms needed the dark. So I came home from camp and threw the bag into the pantry closet

A few weeks later when I opened the closet door to get food for the cats, I saw the bag and realized that it wasn't growing well. So I brought it upstairs and placed it in the bathtub of the bathroom that we use infrequently. I left the bag there for a couple of weeks and the spawn began to grow into a thick mycelium mass, possibly because there is a skylight in the bathroom. A week or so later Rick, my husband, went to run the bath for our son Shane and asked, "What are you letting rot here in the bathtub?" He threw the bag in the sink and I promptly forgot about it again.

As I walked by the bathroom a few days later I noticed that there were oyster mushrooms growing out of the bag. I hadn't done anything to it. I harvested some and then let the bag get dry. I unintentionally ended up with dried mushrooms.

This year, I've followed all the instructions, including making a tent for the bags and misting them daily after they began to fruit. What a treat to have freshly harvested mushrooms, straight from the growing chamber in my bathtub. But please don't tell anybody about this.

Roasted Potato, Mushroom and Asparagus Salad

Serves 4-6

R oasting brings out the flavors of vegetables. This potato salad becomes a complete meal with the addition of beans and other vegetables. When new potatoes are around in June and July, this is incredible. If you can't get good asparagus then, substitute green beans.

2	**pounds small new potatoes or larger potatoes, cut into bite size pieces**
1	**pound crimini mushrooms**
1	**pound thin asparagus**
1-2	**tablespoons olive oil**
1/4	**cup finely chopped roasted red pepper**
1	**cup garbanzo beans, rinsed and drained if canned**

Salt and pepper

1	**tablespoon Dijon mustard**
3	**tablespoons extra virgin olive oil**
2	**tablespoons sherry vinegar**
1	**tablespoon fresh minced tarragon**
2	**tablespoons fresh minced Italian parsley**

Preheat oven to 450° F.

Trim the tops off the beets but leave the tails. Rub the beets with a little oil. Put in a baking dish with the 1/4 cup water. Cover the dish and put in the oven. Test for doneness by inserting a sharp knife after 30 minutes. They may take up to 1 hour to cook, depending on their size. When they are done, let them cool a bit, then peel them and cut them either into rounds, half-rounds or chunks. Season with salt and pepper.

Break the ends off the asparagus, or peel if desired. Toss lightly with oil and lay out on a baking sheet. Roast in the oven for 8 to 10 minutes, until done. Remove from oven, let cool a bit and either leave whole or cut into pieces. Season with salt and pepper.

Put the greens down on a serving platter or in individual plates.

Combine the dressing ingredients - the orange juice through tarragon. Dress the beets and asparagus. Arrange over the greens. Serve with the vegetables warm or chilled.

Wilted Lemon Spinach

Serves 4

I just love the combination of lemon, garlic and spinach. This is so easy to make, except for washing the spinach, but that is easily solved by purchasing the spinach in bags.

1	**large bunch of spinach, about 12 cups of leaves**
1	**tablespoon extra virgin olive oil**
1-2	**cloves garlic, minced**
2	**stalks chopped green garlic, if available**
2	**teaspoons fresh lemon juice**

Salt and pepper

Wash the spinach well by running water over spinach while filling the sink. Rinse well. Lift the spinach leaves from the sink and drain off all the remaining sediment. Wash again, then dry but not thoroughly so there is a bit of water clinging to the leaves.

Heat the oil in a large sauté pan over medium heat. Add the garlic and lemon juice and sauté for 1 minute. Turn the heat to high and add the spinach, 1/4 teaspoon salt and some freshly ground pepper. Wilt the spinach, tossing with tongs to coat with the hot oil and garlic. Serve immediately.

Did You Say Green Onions?

Perhaps where you live green onions are called scallions. They are a member of the allium family, which also includes bulb onions, leeks, garlic, shallots and chives. When the shoots are young and tender they often look similar.

One time I went to New Orleans for a food technology conference - to find a convention hall filled with artificial flavors, colors. starches, gums, additives and very little that resembled food. I yearned for something fresh and couldn't wait to get home to real food.

I was eager to arrive at the San Francisco airport and be back on familiar turf. Rick was in the car waiting for me at the curb when I walked outside the terminal.

I threw my bags in the back seat and sat down in the front next to Rick. I noticed that he didn't smell like his usual self. He reeked of garlic. Rick likes garlic and will eat it but avoids eating it raw or in copious amounts. Since I arrived in the morning I was surprised at the stench. As politely as I could, I asked, "What did you have for dinner last night?"

"I made a salad and put in that bunch of green onions that you had in the frig," he replied.

I laughed, "That explains it. You cut up an entire bunch of green garlic and ate it on your salad last night. You really smell like garlic." He was completely unaware. I often tell my students this story so that they have some warning.

So, be sure that you can tell the difference between green onions and green garlic. Obviously it was easy for Rick to confuse the two since he doesn't buy the food or make the salad. Usually if you crush a leaf and sniff you will know. If you're still not sure, taste it. But don't worry if you confuse them because someone will let you know, hopefully politely.

Carrots with Honey, Lime and Dill

Serves 4

I consider the carrot an underappreciated vegetable even though everyone knows what it is. Carrots are taken for granted. They taste great combined with citrus. Be sure to zest the lime before juicing it. A microplane™ grater works well for this. This treatment turns them into a special side dish.

1   **pound of carrots**
1   **tablespoon honey**
2   **tablespoons lime juice**
1   **teaspoon lime zest**
Vegetable cooking spray
2   **tablespoons water**
2   **teaspoons chopped fresh dill**

Peel carrots and thinly slice on the diagonal.

Combine honey, lime juice and zest and set aside.

Spray a skillet with cooking spray. Add carrots and cook over medium heat, adding water after about 3 minutes or when carrots begin to stick to pan. Cook until carrots are just fork tender. Add honey mixture and stir to coat. Remove from heat and sprinkle with dill. Serve hot.

What's Up, Doc?

"I had so many carrots in my lunch today that I felt like Bugs Bunny," exclaimed my husband Rick. Truth is, I only cut up two large carrots but they were almost equivalent to what you'd find in a bag of "baby" carrots, except that they taste way better.

Rick is a perfect example of someone who has experienced what I like to call "vegetable enlightenment."

When we were first dating, about 15 years ago, he invited me over. He said, "You bring the pizza and I'll make the salad." When I saw Rick's version of salad - iceberg lettuce, a rock hard tomato, some sliced cucumber and a bit of chopped green pepper, I had to give him some credit, but not much. If that was his best attempt at salad I figured that we had no future together.

But over the years I've managed to upgrade Rick's salad. First I switched to romaine lettuce. Then I began to mix in some mesclun or salad mix with a variety of dark greens. Rick occasionally reminds me to leave out the weeds (arugula, dandelion and other bitter greens which are my favorite part) and put in more lettuce. Often I comply by augmenting my own salad with the bitters.

I serve salad with dinner almost every night. And I've noticed that the size of the bowl has been getting larger. Often we need discussion and compromise over who gets to finish the last of the bowl. I never envisioned this conversation but Rick has proven to me that eating vegetables can become a way of life for anyone and everyone -- with the right amount of encouragement.

Asparagus with Black Bean Sauce

Serves 4

*A*sparagus works well to many different flavorings. I love asparagus so can eat it almost nightly when it's in season. Flavored this way, it's great served with Asian-spiced quinoa and baked tofu on the side.

1	**bunch of asparagus, about 1 pound**
1	**tablespoon fermented black beans, rinsed**
2	**cloves garlic, minced**
1	**small piece ginger root, minced**
2	**teaspoons sesame oil**
2	**tablespoons reduced sodium tamari**
2	**tablespoons rice wine vinegar**
1	**tablespoon arrowroot mixed with 1 tablespoon water**

Vegetable cooking spray
Water or broth, as needed

Break off tough asparagus stems. Slice into 2-inch diagonal pieces.

Combine black beans with garlic and ginger. Mash with the back of a spoon to combine.

Spray skillet with vegetable spray. Add asparagus and black bean mixture. Cook for 2 to 3 minutes over medium-high heat. (Add water as needed to prevent sticking.) Then add sesame oil, tamari and rice wine vinegar. Cook for another minute or 2 until asparagus is almost done. Add arrowroot mixture. Stir until it thickens. Serve immediately while hot.

Roasted Baby Leeks a La Nicoise

Serves 4 to 6

*L*eeks are often overlooked in this country. They have a terrific flavor, especially when roasted. If you really like them, as I do, you may need to increase the number of leeks per serving. Roasting without oil is difficult as the oil is what helps the vegetables get a bit caramelized. You can do it with just a tablespoon or two of broth or wine and they will taste good, but just won't brown much.

8-12	**baby leeks about 1/4-inch in diameter, washed well, top few inches of green removed**
1	**tablespoon olive oil**
2	**teaspoons fresh thyme or**
3/4	**teaspoon dried thyme**

Salt and pepper, to taste

2	**tablespoons red wine vinegar**
2	**cloves garlic, minced**
1	**cup peeled, chopped, fresh or canned tomatoes**

Pinch of cayenne pepper
Fresh thyme and chopped Italian parsley, for garnish

Preheat oven to 350° F.

Put the leeks on a baking sheet and drizzle the olive oil over them. Sprinkle the thyme on top of leeks and move them around to be sure that they are coated with oil.

Bake in the oven for 20 minutes until they are getting browned.

While the leeks are roasting, combine the red wine vinegar, garlic, tomatoes and cayenne. After 20 minutes of roasting, add the liquid mixture to the leeks and bake another 10 minutes.

Serve hot, sprinkled with thyme and parsley.

Braised Baby Artichokes with White Wine, Shallots and Garlic

Serves 4

*B*aby artichokes require a bit of work but seem like a better return on labor than the large kind, since you can eat the entire thing. Get small ones as they are the most tender.

5	tablespoons lemon juice
16	baby artichokes
3	tablespoons olive oil
1/2	cup chopped shallots
6	cloves garlic, minced
1/2	cup dry white wine
1/2	teaspoon salt
1/4	teaspoon freshly ground black pepper
3	tablespoons chopped Italian parsley or
1	tablespoon

fresh thyme leaves

Trim the artichokes by having a bowl of acidulated water (with 3 tablespoons lemon juice to 1 quart of water) ready.

Break off any tough outer leaves of the artichoke until you get to the tender, pale leaves. Cut off the top of the artichoke. You can trim the stem but usually on the baby artichokes it is tender enough to eat. As you prepare each artichoke drop it in the water bowl.

When all the artichokes have been prepared, bring a pot of water to a boil. Add the remaining 2 tablespoons of lemon juice. Add the artichokes and cook 2 minutes. Removing and draining them immediately.

Heat the olive oil in a medium skillet over medium heat. Add the shallots and sauté for 3 minutes. Add the artichokes and garlic and sauté for another 3 minutes, until the artichokes start to brown. Add the wine and simmer for at least 5 minutes, until the wine is reduced by about half. Add the salt and pepper. Remove from the heat and sprinkle with the parsley. You can serve this hot, warm or at room temperature.

Serve with chunks of bread so you can sop up all the pan juices.

Green Garlic

Minted Pea Soup

Serves 4-6

*T*his soup is refreshing and cooling, perfect for warmer weather. It only takes several minutes in the pressure cooker or 30 minutes on top of the stove.

1	tablespoon canola oil
1 1/2	cups chopped onions
1	cup diced new potatoes
1	cup peeled and chopped apples
3	cloves garlic, peeled and cut in half
2	bay leaves
1/2	teaspoon dried tarragon
1/2	teaspoon salt
3	cups water
2	cups fresh or frozen peas (reserving a few for garnish)
2	green leaf lettuce leaves
3	tablespoons chopped fresh Italian parsley
1	cup soy milk
1-2	teaspoons fresh lemon juice, or to taste
2	tablespoons fresh chopped mint

Stovetop: Add the oil to a soup pot over medium heat. Sauté the onions for about 7 minutes, until translucent. Add the potatoes, apples, garlic, bay leaves, tarragon, salt and water and simmer for 20 minutes. Add the peas and place the lettuce leaves on top of peas. Simmer another 10 minutes. Remove the bay leaves. Add the parsley to the hot soup and puree until smooth. Stir in the milk, lemon juice and chopped mint. Adjust seasonings, adding more salt, lemon juice or mint. Chill for at least 1 hour. Garnish with whole peas and serve.

Pressure Cooker: Sauté the onion for 5 minutes over medium heat. Add the potatoes, apples, garlic, bay leaves, tarragon, salt and water. Lock the lid on and bring to high pressure. Lower heat to maintain high pressure for 5 minutes. Quick release the pressure. Add the peas and lettuce leaves. Return to high pressure for 3 minutes. Quick release the pressure. Add the parsley and puree until smooth. Stir in the milk, lemon juice and chopped mint. Adjust seasonings, adding more salt, lemon juice or mint. Chill for at least 1 hour. Garnish with whole peas and serve.

Potato and Watercress Soup with Sorrel Cream

Serves 4-6

I never had potato soup that I didn't like. The additional ingredients are perfect for spring as you get the bitter from the watercress and the sour from the sorrel which are useful for "spring cleaning" your body. The soup is creamy and refreshing.

1	tablespoon olive oil
1	medium onion, diced
2	leeks, cleaned and cut into small pieces
1 1/2	pounds Yukon gold or yellow Finn potatoes, peeled and cut into small dice
4	cups vegetable stock or water
1-2	teaspoons salt (only if using water)
2	cups chopped watercress, thick stems removed
1	cup chopped sorrel
	Fresh ground pepper
1/4	cup fresh dill

Cream:

1	package Mori-Nu lite firm or extra firm silken tofu
1	tablespoon fresh lemon juice
1	tablespoon canola or olive oil
2	teaspoons rice vinegar
1/4	teaspoon salt
1	cup chopped sorrel

Heat the oil in a medium pot over medium heat. Add the onions and leeks and sauté for about 8 minutes, until they start to soften. Add the potatoes and stock and bring to a boil. Reduce the heat to a simmer. (If using water, add salt now.) Simmer for 20 minutes, or until the potatoes are tender.

Remove the pot from the heat. Puree a bit with a hand (immersion) blender, until it is your desired consistency. Stir in the watercress, sorrel and pepper. Taste and add more salt if desired. Stir in the dill. Top with the sorrel cream.

While the soup is cooking, make the "cream" by placing all the ingredients for the cream except the sorrel into the food processor. Process until smooth. Taste and adjust seasonings. Pulse in the sorrel. Chill for a bit, up to a day. Drizzle over the hot soup.

Asparagus, Oyster Mushroom and Tofu Stir Fry

Serves 4-6

Get the freshest asparagus you can since it is the star in this dish.

1/2	**pound of extra firm tofu, cut into cubes**
1	**tablespoons tamari or soy sauce**
1	**tablespoon canola oil**
2	**medium shallots, chopped fine**
2	**teaspoons finely minced ginger**
1	**pound of oyster mushrooms,**
	cut in half or more depending on their size
1	**pound of asparagus**
1/2	**teaspoon salt**
1/4	**cup vegetable broth**
1/2	**teaspoon cornstarch or arrowroot**
Finely ground black pepper, to taste	
1	**teaspoon lemon zest**
Lemon juice, to taste	

Marinate the tofu in the tamari while you prepare the other ingredients.

Break off the tough ends of the asparagus and cut the asparagus on the diagonal into 1-inch pieces, except for the tips, which you will leave whole.

In a small bowl, combine the broth, cornstarch, pepper and lemon zest.

Heat the oil over medium high heat in a large skillet or wok. Add the shallots and ginger and sauté for a minute, stirring often. Add the mushrooms and sauté for 5 minutes until they are starting to get limp but are not yet cooked through. Add the tofu, any unabsorbed tamari and the asparagus. Sauté for 3-4 minutes, stirring occasionally. When the mushrooms have released their liquid and the asparagus is bright green and almost cooked through stir the broth mixture and pour into the pan. Stir well to coat all the ingredients. Taste. Add lemon juice, salt or pepper, if necessary.

Serve hot over rice, quinoa or noodles.

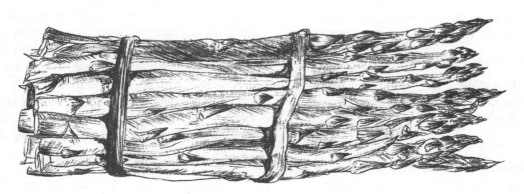

Aspargus

Greek Stuffed Artichokes

Serves 4 as a main course

If I am going to take the time to cook artichokes, I want them to be something more substantial than just a vegetable that I dip into butter or mayonnaise. In this dish, I combine some of my favorite flavors with artichokes to create the centerpiece of a meal.

4	medium artichokes
1	lemon
2	tablespoons assorted chopped, fresh herbs
2	cloves garlic, minced
1 1/2	cups water
1/2	cup dry white wine
1/4	cup olive oil
1	bay leaf
Salt and pepper	

Stuffing:

2	cups fresh bread crumbs
2	tablespoons miso paste
4	ounces firm tofu, crumbled
4	cloves garlic, minced
1/3	cup chopped toasted walnuts
2	tablespoons chopped fresh herbs - basil, thyme, rosemary
2	tablespoons chopped Italian parsley
2	tablespoons grated soy Parmesan cheese
2	tablespoons olive oil
2	tablespoons chopped Italian parsley, for garnish

Trim artichokes:

Cut off artichoke stems and discard. Cut off top 1/2 inch of 1 artichoke with a serrated knife, and then cut about 1/2 inch off all remaining leaf tips with kitchen shears. Rub cut leaves with a lemon half.

Cook artichokes:

Put water, wine, oil, onion, garlic, salt, and pepper in pressure cooker (without insert) or pot and arrange artichokes in liquid in 1 layer.

Seal pressure cooker with lid and cook at high pressure, according to manufacturer's instructions, 6-8 minutes. Put pressure cooker in sink (do not remove lid) and run cold water over lid until pressure goes down completely.

If using a regular pot, simmer artichokes, covered, until leaves are tender, about 50 minutes.

Reserve the cooking liquid.

Make stuffing:

While the artichokes are cooking, make the stuffing.

Preheat oven to 350°F.

Spread breadcrumbs in a shallow baking pan and bake in middle of oven until pale golden, about 10 minutes. Cool crumbs completely, then combine with the miso, tofu, garlic, herbs, parsley and walnuts.

Stuff artichokes:

Let artichokes cool slightly.

Separate leaves slightly with your thumbs and using a spoon, scoop out purple leaves from center and enough yellow leaves to expose fuzzy choke. Scoop out choke with a spoon or melon-ball cutter, and then squeeze some lemon juice into cavity.

Trim remaining artichokes in same manner.

Spoon about 3-4 tablespoons stuffing into cavity of each artichoke and, starting with bottom leaves and spreading leaves open as much as possible without breaking, spoon a rounded 1/2 teaspoon stuffing inside each leaf. Arrange the artichokes in a baking dish and sprinkle each artichoke with grated soy Parmesan cheese and drizzle with olive oil. Pour the leftover artichoke cooking liquid into the bottom of the baking dish.

Cover with parchment and then foil.

Bake at 350° F. for 25 minutes. Remove foil and parchment and brown under the broiler for a minute or two. Serve hot, garnished with parsley.

Who Ever Thought?

I cannot imagine who might have ever thought about picking an artichoke, letting alone eating it. And then how the heck did they ever get through the thorns on the outside leaves to discover an inner core that tastes great? It makes me wonder about how hungry some people must have been compared to today with our modern supermarkets, sometimes open 24 hours a day. Today the hungry people are not eating artichokes, because preparing the thorny thistles still requires work.

For those who love artichokes, they are worth the trouble. I like them, but no one else in my family does, so I don't make them that often. I do use them in my classes, since most people want to learn how to deal with this thistle-flower.

I find that kitchen scissors work well for trimming artichoke leaves and a knife can access the stem and bottom. I don't often just make artichoke hearts since it seems like such a waste of plant material. The bottoms of the more inner leaves are delicious, either when prepared stuffed, as in this recipe, or when dipped into something with garlic and lemon, such as a dip.

I have found two items that taste as good or better than large artichokes. They are the baby artichokes that have not yet developed their choke, or spikes on the leaves, and a new type of artichoke that is tinged purple and called a French artichoke. I found it mostly thorn- and choke-free with good flavor similar to the baby artichoke.

Artichokes, like most vegetables, are best when they are eaten in season. Luckily, here in California, the season is a long one, beginning late winter, and going through the fall. They show up at other times, too but are best in spring. If you've never tried artichokes, it's time.

Artichokes

Pea and Asparagus Risotto

Serves 4-6

*R*isotto has gained a place on restaurant menus in recent years, but it is really simple food. Adding asparagus and peas shows off fresh spring veggies. This recipe adapts easily to any fresh vegetables.

1	tablespoon oil
1	cup chopped leeks or onion
2	cloves garlic, minced plus 2 stalks green garlic, if available
1 1/2	cups Arborio rice

A pinch of saffron, soaked in 1 tablespoon hot water
4 1/2-5 cups of boiling stock or water
    with broth powder or paste

1/2	cup white wine such as Sauvignon Blanc
1/2	teaspoon salt
1	cup fresh shelled peas or frozen thawed peas
1	cup asparagus stalks and tops, cut into small pieces
1/3	cup grated soy Parmesan cheese
2	tablespoons coarsely chopped Italian parsley

Have the stock in a pot on the stove and have it simmering on a burner near where you will cook your risotto.

Heat the olive oil in a saucepan over medium heat. Add the leeks and sauté for 2 minutes. Then add the garlic and sauté another minute. Add the rice and stir well to coat it with the oil.

Add the saffron and its soaking water and begin adding the stock, a cup at a time, allowing the rice to absorb each cup of stock completely before adding more. Keep stirring.

When the rice has absorbed 3 cups of stock, add the wine, if using, and the salt. Continue to add the stock, stirring constantly, until there is about a cup left; this will take 15 to 20 minutes. Add the remaining stock, peas, asparagus and some pepper. Taste the rice. It should be a bit firm and the sauce kind of soupy and the asparagus ought to be tender-crisp. Stir in the cheese. Top with parsley. Serve with additional cheese.

Fasoulia

Serves 4

*T*his Greek dish is usually made with either fava beans or large white beans common in the region. I use dried cannellini or fava beans. The fava beans have an outer skin that must be removed after soaking, so they are more work. Butter beans or any other large white bean also substitutes well. I am sure that you can make a similar recipe with fresh fava beans but I've decided that they are too much work so usually avoid them.

2	cups dried cannellini or fava beans, presoaked
5	cups water to cover and cook
2	medium Yukon Gold or Yellow Finn potatoes, diced
6	cloves garlic, minced
1	bay leaf
3	tablespoons tomato paste
1	teaspoon dried oregano

Salt and freshly ground pepper, to taste

2-3	tablespoons fresh squeezed lemon juice
3	tablespoons chopped fresh Italian parsley

Add the beans, water, potatoes, garlic and bay leaf to a large saucepan. Bring the mixture to a boil, then reduce the heat to a simmer. Simmer for 30 to 40 minutes or more until the beans are cooked through. (The time at this point will depend upon the age of the beans.) Then add the tomato paste and oregano and cook until the liquid turns into a thick tomato puree.

Remove from the heat, take out the bay leaf and add the lemon juice. Taste and add salt and pepper, if desired.

Serve hot or at room temperature, garnished with Italian parsley.

Mediterranean French Green Lentils

Serves 4 to 6

*I*nspired by a recipe by Martha Rose Shulman in Goumet Vegetarian Feasts French lentils are great to use in salads because they remain firm when cooked. This salad is light and lively. It can be served on top of greens or as is. You can also serve it along side a grain salad made with bulgur wheat, quinoa or brown rice. Or you can add some cooked grain to this salad. It's delicious any way that I have ever made it.

1/2	pound French green lentils, about 1 1/4 cups
3-4	cups water
1/2	red onion, sliced thinly into half rounds
1	pound carrots, peeled
2	tablespoons chopped chives
1-2	tablespoons chopped parsley
1/4	cup currants

juice of 1/2 lemon

3	tablespoons freshly squeezed orange juice
3	tablespoons Balsamic vinegar
1	small clove garlic, crushed
1 1/2	teaspoons Dijon mustard
1	tablespoon extra virgin olive oil
1/2	teaspoon ground cumin
1	teaspoon lemon zest
1	teaspoon orange zest

Salt and freshly ground pepper, to taste

Spray a pan with cooking spray. Sauté the onion over medium heat until tender. Add the lentils and water and bring to a boil. Reduce to a simmer, cover and cook 25 to 40 minutes until the lentils are tender but not mushy. Drain and set aside (saving the liquid for another use such as soup or sauce).

Grate carrots by hand or with a food processor. Toss them with chives, parsley and currants.

Combine lemon juice, orange juice, vinegar, garlic, mustard, cumin, lemon and orange zest, salt and pepper (and oil if using). Add lentils and carrots. Combine well. Serve at once.

This salad may also be served chilled.

Full of Beans, Sans Gas

To get beans ready for cooking, sort them to get rid of any cracked or broken beans, stones or dirt. Beans usually need at least a quick visual check to get rid of cracked or broken beans, rocks or other debris. Rinse them under water, then soak them. Since I don't usually remember to soak beans the night before or even in the morning for that evening, I almost always quick soak beans.

Quick soaking seems to penetrate the beans more than other methods, which is why it may make the beans less gassy. Put the beans in a pot and cover with water by at least 3 inches. Bring the water to a boil and boil for 1 minute. Remove the pot from the heat, cover it and let the beans sit for 1 hour. Drain the soaking water from your beans (use it to water plants) and then proceed with cooking on the stove top or in the pressure cooker.

You can choose to forego presoaking and take beans from dry to fully cooked. However, it usually doubles the cooking time and I've found that the beans are unevenly cooked at the end. I consider some form of presoaking essential for well cooked beans. Lentils and peas are the exception as they go from dry to cooked in just 25 to 45 minutes.

Food is our common ground, a universal experience.

James Beard,
Cookbook author, 1903 -1985

Summer

*E*ven though the days of my youth, running barefoot and staying up late are far behind me, the light of summer and the accompanying fresh produce is exhilarating. While spring is rebirth, summer is full birth – spending time outdoors, wearing fewer or smaller clothes, dining on the deck, having impromptu picnics at the park or beach. And then there's the light. The sunshine that teases plants and makes them grow, some sprouting like weeds. Picture a garden of tomatoes, summer squash, cucumbers and corn.

I've found that summer meals involve minor cooking and some assembling, such as piling chopped tomatoes over pasta, sprinkling barely steamed green beans with fresh tarragon or thyme, or removing grilled sweet corn kernels from their cobs into a bowl to turn it into a salad. The vegetables speak for themselves and do not need much help from me. Taking the time to pick the best really pays off now.

Produce is abundant. If my favorite grower is out of squash, the farmer at the next market stall is sure to have some. Heck, there may be a plant or two in my garden this year. Or maybe a friend has grown squash. Many people enjoy growing vegetables and have surplus to share. Ask everyone you know if you can be the recipient of his or her homegrown veggies. You'll find a number of recipes for zucchini and other squash.

When it's hot, staying out of the kitchen is as important as what we eat. Choose lots of salads, raw vegetables and lightly cooked foods. Learn to use a pressure cooker, a grill or barbecue. Let your summer eating remind you of the joys of sunny summer.

Eggplant "Caviar"

Makes about 1 1/2 - 2 cups

My grandmother used to make a dip like this. Someone in the family has her recipe but this is my closest guess. Hers was better, though.

2	eggplants, about 1 pound each
2	tablespoons olive oil
6	cloves unpeeled garlic
1	tablespoon balsamic vinegar
2	tablespoons capers
2	cloves minced garlic
1/4	cup finely chopped tomatoes, fresh or canned
2	tablespoons chopped Italian parsley
1	teaspoon, or more, Sucanat or sugar

Salt and pepper, to taste

Preheat the oven to 400° F.

Cut each eggplant in half lengthwise, brushing the cut surfaces lightly with olive oil. Place cut side down on a baking sheet. Lightly brush the garlic cloves with oil and put them on the baking sheet. Bake until eggplant and garlic are tender, about 30 to 40 minutes. Remove the eggplant from the pan and let cool. When cool, peel off the skin and coarsely chop the flesh, putting it into a large bowl.

Squeeze the roasted garlic from its skin and mince. Add it to the eggplant.

Mix the olive oil, vinegar, capers, minced garlic, tomatoes and parsley with the eggplant and roasted garlic. Add Sucanat or sugar to taste. The flavor should be a bit sweet and sour. Let sit for an hour at room temperature to let the flavors blend. Taste again before serving and adjust flavors, adding more vinegar or sugar, to taste.

If you prefer a smoother dip, put all the ingredients in the food processor and blend to a puree.

This will last for a few days if you can keep from eating all of it.

Eggplants

Around the Globe with Eggplant

"I just bought a lousy eggplant," my friend Laurie complained the other day.

"Of course you did," I shot back. "It's January. There really isn't any decent eggplant available now. You need to buy it when it's in season, during summer and fall."

I hope that I didn't hurt Laurie's feelings, but I just wanted her to know that eggplant, like all vegetables, is seasonal. She probably spotted decent-looking eggplant at Community Market or another natural foods store and took a shot. This is the problem with global commerce. You see zucchini in December and tomatoes in January coming from faraway places, shipped long distances and most likely picked unripe. Sometimes it is easy to get fooled into thinking something will taste good just because it looks good.

People often ask me how to choose a good eggplant. My response is to know a reputable farmer and then buy their eggplant. If you can't do that, use the following tips.

Eggplant quality quickly goes downhill as it ages. A fresher one that is firm, shiny and without dents or dings is less likely to be spongy. Fresh eggplant can be stored on the countertop for a few days. So use it soon after buying.

The rule of thumb for choosing eggplant is to select one that is heavy for its size. Now, what does that mean? Compare eggplant of similar size and choose the heavier one.

There are many types, shapes, and sizes of eggplant. Most can be used in a stir-fry type dish or a sauté, but not all will work on the grill. The eggplant with less flesh will sometimes burn on the grill unless they are roasted whole. The most commonly seen eggplant is the dark purple, large Italian type. There are also smaller Middle Eastern ones that look similar. The slender, long, Asian eggplant can also be grilled.

Eggplants come in a huge variety of colors, including white, bright orange, green, lavender, yellow, striped and more. The size ranges from the size of a golf ball to that of a football. They may be round, narrow, or cylindrical. I have found most of the tiny eggplants to be too seedy and now avoid them.

One year I grew Green Goddess, a green Asian eggplant, which was exceptional. Growing them yourself insures their freshness. Freshly picked eggplant often doesn't need to be salted. I only salt when it helps make the eggplant pliable for a recipe, as in the Szechwan Eggplant Roll-ups. Eggplant tends to get bitter and seedy when they are overripe. If you find a lot of seeds in your large eggplant, cut them out if possible, before proceeding with your recipe.

Since eggplant has little flavor of its own, it acts like a sponge in cooking, taking on whatever seasonings you add, making it easy to jazz it up. I usually marinate it or add a marinade during cooking. It marries well with a host of herbs, spices and flavors from Thai and Chinese to Italian, Greek and Indian. You can bake, roast, grill, fry, stir-fry or sauté eggplant. You can stuff them, put them on salads or pizza or turn roasted pieces into a sandwich filling or dip like Baba Ganouj (a variation on hummus). And ratatouille would not be what it is without eggplant. Try my grilled version on page 33.

Sweet Summer Super Salad

Serves 4 -6

*S*ome people don't like the combination of fruit and vegetables, yet I find the blend of sweet, tangy and bitter flavors to be light and delicious. Use the freshest, most flavorful fruit available -- it makes all the difference. If you want even more flavor contrast, add a few chopped salty olives or capers.

Dressing:

1/4	cup raspberries or strawberries
2	tablespoons raspberry or other fruit vinegar
3	tablespoons water or broth, or oil substitute for salad dressing (see page 93)
2	teaspoons honey or other sweetener
2	teaspoons Dijon mustard
	Freshly ground pepper, to taste

Salad:

4	cups mixed baby lettuce
2	cups arugula or other bitter greens
1/4	cup sliced onions or green onions, use white and green
1	cup summer stone fruit (peaches, apricots, plums, nectarines), sliced
1	small avocado, cut into 12 slices
3	tablespoons toasted sunflower seeds, for garnish
3	tablespoons raspberries or strawberries, for garnish

Combine all dressing ingredients in a small food processor or blender. Puree until well combined. Set aside.

Combine the lettuce, arugula and onions. Mix with the dressing and arrange on a large platter or individual plates.

Place the fruit and avocado on top. Garnish with the sunflower seeds and raspberries.

Floribbean Summer Fruit Salsa Salad

Serves 4 -6

*H*ere the sweetness of peaches and nectarines are combined with vegetables and herbs to produce an unusual and tasty salad with a kick. One of my students asked what a floriBEAN was. I explained that the term stands for Florida (where I went to graduate school) and Caribbean. She was relieved, sure that she would not like this type of bean.

2	peaches, cut into slices, then in half
2	nectarines, cut into slices, then in half
1	avocado, cut in half and then into chunks
1/2	cup cucumber, chopped, seeded and peeled, if necessary
1/2	cup chopped tomatoes or halved cherry tomatoes
1/2	cup chopped red pepper
1	teaspoon grated fresh ginger
2	tablespoons orange juice
2	tablespoons lime juice
1/4	teaspoon salt
2	tablespoons olive oil (optional)
1/4	cup chopped cilantro
1/2-1	jalapeno, finely chopped
2-3	cups washed and dried baby greens

Just before serving, combine the peaches, nectarines, avocado, cucumber, tomatoes and red pepper.

In a separate bowl, blend the ginger, orange juice, lime juice, salt and olive oil.

Sprinkle the cilantro and jalapeno over the mango-avocado mixture. Pour on the dressing and carefully combine.

Divide the greens among 4 to 6 serving plates. Place some of the salsa on top of the greens. Serve immediately.

Mediterranean Bean, Herb and Tomato Salad

Serves 4

*T*here is nothing like summer tomato salads to give "fresh" a new meaning. McDougallers will use broth and a pinch of guar gum or oil substitute, instead of olive oil.

6	cups young greens, washed and dried
1	cup white beans, presoaked or 2 cups cooked or canned beans
3-4	sprigs thyme, savory or other fresh herbs
1 1/2	pounds ripe heirloom or other tomatoes of any variety
1	cup sliced cucumber, cut into half moon shapes
12	pitted Kalamata olives
2	tablespoons chopped fresh basil
1	tablespoon chopped fresh oregano
2	tablespoons chopped fresh Italian parsley
1/2	teaspoon lemon zest
2	tablespoons fresh lemon juice
3	tablespoons extra virgin olive oil
1/4	teaspoon salt

Freshly ground pepper, to taste

Put the greens in the refrigerator to chill.

Cook the beans with the thyme, savory or other herb sprigs until they are cooked through and still firm. Cannellini beans take 30-40 minutes to cook, while white or Great Northern cook in about 1 hour. Or pressure cook for 5 to 8 minutes at high pressure with a natural pressure release. When the beans are cooked, put them in a bowl. If using canned beans, cut the herbs and mix with the lemon marinade below.

While the beans are cooking, cut the tomatoes into wedges. Combine the lemon zest and juice, oil, salt and pepper and pour over the cooked beans. Let this mixture marinate for at least 25 minutes and then add the chopped basil, oregano and parsley to the beans, along with the olives.

Arrange the greens on individual plates. Place one fourth of the bean mixture on the top of greens. Divide cucumbers, olives and tomatoes evenly and place on top of the greens and beans.

Tomatoes

Tomatillo, Summer Vegetable, Brown and Wild Rice Salad

Serves 4-6

*T*omatillos, traditionally used in Mexican cooking, are an underutilized summer vegetable that has to have a tart and crunchy taste. Here they are paired with other summer veggies and Mexican seasonings to make a colorful grain salad.

1	cup brown and wild rice mix, Lundberg Farms makes a good one
2	cups water
1	tablespoon chicken flavored broth powder
1/4	pound Romano, green or wax beans, chopped into 1/4-inch pieces
1	ear corn, kernels removed or 1 cup of corn kernels
1	red pepper, diced
3/4	pound tomatillos - chop half into bite-sized pieces and blend what remains with the garlic, lime juice or vinegar until almost smooth
2	green onions, chopped
3	tablespoons chopped cilantro
1	clove garlic, minced or crushed
2	tablespoons lime juice or mild vinegar

In a 1 1/2 to 2 quart saucepan, boil the water. Stir in the broth powder. Add the rice and reduce the heat to a simmer. Cook, covered, for 40 minutes. Remove from heat. Place the chopped green or yellow beans and corn kernels on top of the rice in the pan and replace cover. Let sit for 5 minutes to steam.

Place the cooked rice in a serving dish. Add the remaining vegetables and cilantro. Toss with the blended tomatillo-vinegar-garlic mixture. Taste and add salt and pepper, if desired. Serve warm or at room temperature.

Note: You can use any vegetables in this dish that look good to you. Another tasty combination is chopped summer squash, corn and tomatoes.

Doubly Red Potato Salad

Makes 8 to 10 servings

I love the color of this potato salad as well as the taste. The addition of salty olives, red onion and dill elevates the simple ingredients of beets and potatoes into another realm.

6	cups quartered small red potatoes (about 2 pounds)
1	pound small red beets, tops trimmed
1	teaspoon salt
1	cup diced red onion (1 large fresh dug spring onion, if available)
1/2	cup minced fresh dill
1/2	cup pitted Kalamata olives, sliced in half lengthwise
1/2	box Mori Nu lite silken extra firm tofu
2	tablespoons white wine vinegar
1/4	cup vegan sour cream or 1/4 cup soy yogurt

Steam the potatoes over boiling water until they are tender, 10 to 12 minutes. Drain and cool.

Cook the beets in boiling water to just cover them, until they are tender, about 12 to 15 minutes. Drain, cool and slip off the skin. Cut the beets into 1-inch cubes.

Gently combine the potatoes and beets in a large bowl, along with the salt, onion, dill and olives.

Put the tofu in the blender with the vinegar. Blend until smooth and pour into a small bowl. Stir the vegan sour cream into the tofu blend and fold into the salad. Chill and serve, or serve at room temperature.

Note: *You can substitute 1/2 cup regular or vegan mayonnaise for the blended tofu mixture.*

Beets

One Potato, Two Potato, Three Potato...

"More please," I say. I love potatoes. All of their different qualities -- earthy, creamy, starchy or waxy -- appeal to me. They are the ultimate comfort food. I like eating them prepared most ways except fried or raw.

The potato's versatility and variety amaze me. You can find them marble-sized, but also the size of softballs. They're all good.

Oh! Tommy Boy's in Petaluma, California grows thirty kinds of potatoes. Some have brown skin and white or gold inside, red skin and innards, purple skin and white flesh, deep purple throughout, pink on the outside and yellow inside, red on the outside and inside and on and on. And the shapes are also as varied from small and round, to irregular, long and narrow or large and oblong, and everything in between.

Some of my favorites are the fingerlings such as Rose Finn Apple or Russian Banana, which are smallish, oddly shaped oblong potatoes that sometimes look like animals when you study them. Shane often helps me pick them out. We agree that we ought to buy the ones that remind of us walruses, seals, horses, pigs or other creatures. In summer or early fall I like coating them with a bit of olive oil and grilling them, or as the weather cools roasting them in the oven. They're the best for grilled potato salads.

I have favorites for mashing, too. I like to use Yukon Gold, German Butterball or Yellow Finn because their golden color and creamy flesh gives the appearance of butter without the fat. But I've also made pink mashed potatoes with Cranberry (All Red) or Huckleberry potatoes; lavender mashed potatoes with Peruvian purples; and my favorite, true purple potatoes with Black Beauty (also called Mollye).

When the July 4th holiday rolls around, I celebrate with Red, White and Blue Potato Salad. Although potatoes are available year round, potatoes do have a season. Here in Northern California they are harvested from August through November, but keep much longer when stored in a cool, dry place. Store your potatoes in paper, not plastic, bags. And do not put them in the refrigerator, which causes the starch to turn to sugar, creating an unpleasant taste and texture.

I don't suggest buying the large 5 or 10-pound plastic bags of potatoes sold at the supermarket unless you plan to use them up quickly. These potatoes tend to hang around in storage for a long time and could give potatoes a bad name. They are usually sprayed with an anti-sprout agent and tend to mold before they sprout.

Sprouting is a sign of age, but if the eyes are just beginning to sprout and the potato is still firm, you can cut or rub off the sprouts and happily eat your potato.

Any green color that you notice on potatoes comes from exposure to light. A substance called solanine causes this. Eaten in large quantities it is poisonous but eating one potato won't likely harm you. If there's just a little bit, cut away the green part. If the potato is all green, throw it away.

Potatoes taste different when they are freshly dug. They are called "new" potatoes and can come in any color. Most often we think of "new" potatoes as red potatoes, but not all red potatoes are new or vice versa. If the skin rubs off easily the potatoes are new. They taste freshest and are great just lightly steamed with a sprinkling of lemon juice and chopped parsley. All this potato talk reminds me that I need some comforting and potatoes are perfect for that. I just need to decide what kind.

Andean Corn and Quinoa Salad

Serves 4-6

Quinoa is so nutritious. It is the staple grain of the Andes Mountains in Peru. Here it is combined with corn to make a complete meal. It tastes great when you make it and the flavors hold up well for the next day.

1	cup quinoa
1 3/4	cups water
1	tablespoon chicken flavored or veggie broth powder
1/2	teaspoon salt
1	tablespoon canola oil
1	medium onion, diced
1 1/2	cups fresh or frozen, thawed corn
2	cloves garlic, minced
2	teaspoons cumin
1	teaspoon coriander powder
1	large red pepper, diced
1	jalapeño, minced
3	tablespoons chopped cilantro, or more to taste
1	medium tomato, diced
2	tablespoons chopped parsley
3	tablespoons lime juice

Salt and pepper, to taste

Rinse the quinoa well in a fine mesh sieve. Heat a saucepan over medium heat. Add the quinoa and toast for 1-2 minutes, until it is dry. Add the water and chicken flavored broth powder. Bring to a boil, reduce the heat to a simmer and cover. Cook for 12 minutes. Remove from the heat and let sit for 5 minutes. Remove the cover and stir in the salt. Put into a bowl and chill.

Add the oil to a sauté pan over medium heat. Add the onions and corn and sauté for 7 minutes. Add the garlic, cumin, coriander, red pepper and jalapeño and cook for 5 more minutes, until the peppers are cooked through but still firm. Remove the pan from the heat and stir in the cilantro, tomato and parsley. Put the mixture in a medium bowl and chill for 15 minutes. After 15 minutes in the refrigerator, stir the vegetables and lime juice into the quinoa. Taste and adjust the seasonings. Serve chilled or at room temperature.

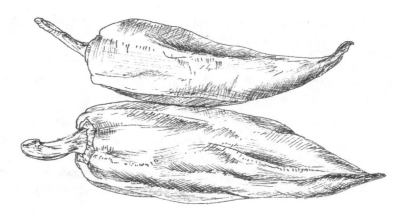

Jalopeños

Honey Mustard Green Bean and Bulgur Salad

Serves 4-6

*T*here is something so delicious about fresh green beans when they are cooked until tender-crisp. Combined with grains and maybe some cooked kidney, white or garbanzo beans, this can be a hearty side dish or the highlight of the meal.

1 1/2	cups vegetable broth
1	cup bulgur wheat
1	pound green, wax or purple beans, cut in half
4	tablespoons honey mustard
2	tablespoons freshly squeezed orange juice
1	tablespoon rice wine vinegar
1	tablespoon olive oil
1/4- 1/2	teaspoon salt
1/4	teaspoon freshly ground black pepper
1	cup cooked beans, any kind (optional)
2	tablespoons chopped Italian parsley

Bring the broth to a boil and pour over the bulgur in a medium bowl. Let sit for at least 20 minutes, or until the bulgur has absorbed the broth.

Steam the green beans over water for 5 to 7 minutes, until they are bright green and still somewhat firm but cooked through. Remove from the heat and put in a metal bowl in the refrigerator to chill.

Meanwhile, combine the honey mustard, orange juice, vinegar and olive oil in a small bowl. Add the salt and pepper and mix well.

Combine the chilled green beans and the cooked beans, if using, with the bulgur. Pour on the dressing and mix well. Taste and adjust seasonings. Garnish with the Italian parsley.

Pull Over, Please

I don't need much provocation to drive off the road. Er, I mean pull off the road. Any sign proclaiming fresh picked produce (of any kind) and you'll find me flipping on my turn signal and carefully stopping on the shoulder.

Just this morning I drove by a large wooden sign proclaiming fresh green beans and eggplant. I was disappointed because the stand was closed. Luckily, on my trip home, the vegetables were visible, beckoning me to stop. The gentleman selling produce was also the farmer. He told me that everything was just picked.

After he handed me the bag containing my purchases, I snatched a green bean and took a bite. "Oh, crisp and delicious," I proclaimed, loudly enough for the other customers to hear. Why not help him boost his sales and let others benefit from the bounty?

Whether on a country lane or a major freeway, an advertisement for a farm stand, or fresh grown anything, is an invitation for me to take a detour and have a food adventure. When visiting Maine a number of years ago, I saw a sign on the side of the road for blueberries. (I know this is a vegetable book but...) I didn't even ask my husband if it was OK to stop there. I pulled over. Getting out of the car, I was excited by the prospect of my favorite fruit. I bought an entire shoe box full of sweet wild blueberries for two dollars. I ate blueberries every day for the entire week. I didn't even share.

Sometimes we get a sign to stop for fresh produce. Usually it pays off.

Italian Bread Salad

Serves 6

*T*he time to make this is when the tomatoes are ripe, calling your name and it's hot outside. It won't work with fresh bread so make sure that you've got some stale bread around or buy it specifically to make this. Bread with herbs or garlic is especially good.

1	**pound stale sourdough or whole grain bread, flavored is good**
1	**small red onion**
1	**large garlic clove**
2-3	**large tomatoes**
1-2	**tablespoons Dijon mustard**
4	**tablespoons Balsamic vinegar**
1	**tablespoon olive oil**
1	**cup assorted cherry tomatoes**
2	**tablespoons chopped fresh basil**
2	**tablespoons chopped fresh parsley**
	Salt and freshly ground pepper, to taste
2	**tablespoons soy Parmesan**

Cut the bread into cubes and let stand exposed while making the salad.

Slice the onion into thin rings.

Plunge the large tomatoes into boiling water for 30 seconds. Peel, core and cut into quarters. In a food processor, finely chop garlic. Add tomatoes and process until smooth. Add mustard, vinegar and oil. Process to incorporate. Combine the blended tomato mixture with the bread, cherry tomatoes, basil and parsley.

Add salt and pepper to taste.

Refrigerate for a couple of hours before serving. Serve chilled, sprinkled with soy cheese.

Grilled Asian Squash Salad

Serves 4

*W*hen the squash is prolific, you always need another way to serve it. This dish is especially easy and delicious. Even people who say they don't like squash usually find it irresistible.

1	**tablespoon olive oil**
1	**teaspoon sesame oil**
2	**tablespoons rice wine vinegar**
1	**tablespoon reduced sodium tamari**
4	**summer squash of any kind, cut lengthwise into quarters**
1	**large onion, cut into rings**
3	**tablespoons chopped herbs, such as cilantro, Thai basil or parsley**
2-3	**cloves garlic, minced**
1	**teaspoon grated ginger**
	Chopped cilantro or other herb, for garnish
	Salt and pepper to taste

Combine olive oil, sesame oil, vinegar, tamari and half the garlic and ginger in a bowl or zippered bag. Mix in squash, onion and herbs. Let marinate at least 30 minutes to 1 hour.

Place veggies on a screen on your grill over hot coals or gas or inside on a grill pan. Grill for 3-4 minutes on each side. Turn carefully and grill for another 3-4 minutes on the other side. Reserve the marinade. Once the squash is grilled, cut it into bite-sized pieces. Mix with cooked onion rings, reserved marinade and remaining ginger and garlic. Add salt and pepper to taste. Garnish with chopped cilantro. Serve as is, or cool to room temperature.

On the Prowl

I admit it. I can't commit. Unlike some people who find it easy to be faithful to one farmer by joining their CSA (Consumer Supported Agriculture) subscription program and paying up front to keep the farm solvent, I prefer to carouse and philander. I'm out hoping for the thrill of a lifetime - a new variety of vegetable offered first to me.

I've been disappointed by farmers before. If I need 15 pounds of eggplant next Wednesday, it won't do if there are only 10 pounds, or if the farmer forgets to bring them to the market. Therefore, I can't commit, and don't want to.

I troll the farmer's market and local farm stands, looking for the crème de la crème of vegetables, as fresh as they can be. Sometimes they aren't even for a recipe, but for audience show and tell or a photo shoot. They've got to be at their peak quality and appearance.

I'll go out of my way to find a hidden gem - drive for miles down dirt roads if I hear of something worth seeking.

The younger Larry of Triple T Ranch and Farm jokes about how I don't spend much money with them. I explain that I've got to spread my money around, just like love. Give them just enough so they want me to come back, yet I won't promise to marry them for fear of not getting what I want.

Don't worry about me. My husband is well aware of my ways. That's because he loves being able to eat the best vegetables I can get.

Next...

Summer Squash "Vichyssoise"

Serves 6

I like this soup because it tastes so fresh, is low in fat and can be served hot or cold.

2	teaspoons olive or canola oil
1	cup chopped onion
3	cloves garlic, minced
1 1/2	cups diced new potatoes
3 1/2	cups water
1/2	tablespoon chicken flavored or vegetable broth powder
4	cups sliced summer squash, use a mixture of pattypan, zucchini, scallopini, crookneck or Ronde de Nice
1/2	cup chopped basil
1	cup multigrain, rice or soy milk

Salt and freshly ground pepper, to taste
Basil sprigs, for garnish

Heat the oil in a large pot. Add the onion and cook over medium heat for 2 minutes. Put in the potatoes and about 1/4 cup water to keep the vegetables from sticking. Cook for about 10 minutes, adding more water if necessary. Add the remaining water, broth powder and squash. Stir well and bring to a boil. Reduce the heat and simmer for 5 minutes. Add the basil and cook another 5 minutes or until the squash is soft. Blend with an immersion blender or in the blender or food processor, in 2 batches, until smooth. Return to the pot, if using a blender or processor. Add the milk and heat through. Serve immediately or chill and serve cold. Garnish with basil sprigs.

Chilled Cucumber Dill Soup

Serves 4

There is something so incredibly refreshing about the combination of cucumbers and dill. Chilling the soup amplifies the effect even more.

3	**medium cucumbers**
1	**tablespoon chopped fresh dill**
2	**teaspoons Dijon mustard**
1/2	**teaspoon sherry or champagne vinegar**
2	**tablespoons vegan sour cream**

Freshly ground black pepper

1	**teaspoon mustard or cumin seeds, toasted**
1/2	**teaspoon salt**
5	**red radishes, trimmed and chopped**

Sprigs of dill, for garnish

Peel the cucumbers and cut them in half lengthwise. Scoop out the seeds with a teaspoon and dice the cucumbers. Transfer the cucumbers to a blender or food processor. Add the dill, mustard, vinegar, sour cream and pepper. Puree until it is completely smooth. Transfer to a mixing bowl and refrigerate until chilled.

Heat a small skillet over medium heat. Add the mustard seeds and toast them until they turn gray, taking care to not burn them. You may need to partially cover the pan to keep the seeds from jumping out. Remove them from the heat and let cool.

Just before serving, stir half the chopped radishes into the soup. Ladle the soup into shallow rimmed plates. Sprinkle with the remaining radishes, sprigs of dill and the mustard seeds.

Smoky Gazpacho

Serves 4

This recipe deviates from traditional gazpacho, but is even perkier. Choose large, ripe tomatoes with plenty of acidity. Avoid the yellow or orange type tomatoes, as they are too sweet for this soup.

1	**medium sized cucumber**
3	**pounds vine ripe tomatoes (about 4 large) or 1 28-oz can whole peeled tomatoes**
1/2	**cup red onion, diced**
1	**jalapeno pepper, seeded and thinly sliced**
1	**dried chipotle pepper, seeds removed, minced fine or ground**
1/4	**cup fresh chopped cilantro**
2-3	**cloves garlic, crushed**
1/2	**teaspoon salt**

Freshly ground black pepper, to taste

2	**tablespoons mild vinegar, such as rice vinegar**
2	**teaspoons lime juice**

Peel the cucumber. Scoop out the seeds and dice. Set aside.

Bring a large pot of water to a boil. Drop the tomatoes into the boiling water a few at a time for about 10 seconds, just long enough to loosen their skins. Scoop the tomatoes out of the water. Run under cold water to cool, then slip off their skins.

Place a mesh strainer over a bowl. Cut the tomatoes in half crosswise. Hold the tomato over the strainer, squeeze out the juice and seeds, saving the pulp. Discard the seeds and save the juice for the soup. Puree half the tomato pulp and cucumbers with all the tomato juice in the blender or food processor. Coarsely chop the rest of the tomatoes by hand. Combine the blended tomatoes and cucumber with the onion, jalapeno, chipotle, cilantro, salt and garlic in a large bowl. Season with vinegar, lime juice and pepper.

Refrigerate for at least an hour. Add more vinegar, salt, pepper or lime juice, if needed. Serve chilled.

Note: *If you find that the soup is too acidic, add a few pinches of sugar or drops of stevia.*

Variety on Your Plate at the Farmer's Market

If you don't know an English cucumber from an Armenian, use the farm market as a learning experience. You might also find Japanese cucumbers, Middle Eastern Painted Serpents and the tiny, prickly West Indies gherkins. When you investigate squash you'll find it in colors from yellow to light green (called grey), to dark green, and in shapes from the size of your thumb to that of a Little League bat, once again from all corners of the world.

And who could live without tomatoes that truly taste like tomatoes? Tomatoes come in every shade of the rainbow, from white to yellow, orange, pink, purple, green and red. There's even one called Blue Fruit but, alas, it isn't really blue. The names alone could keep you pondering about their origins — Cherokee Purple, Mortgage Lifter, Aunt Ruby's German, Green Zebra. They're all heirlooms, varieties of the past. Tomato flavors run the gamut from sweet to acidic, and all are juicy. Once you try them, you'll either come back to the market to buy more, or grow your own next year.

Farm fresh produce lasts longer than that sold in the grocery store, since it travels directly from the farm to you without a stop at a warehouse or back room. When I buy what looks good, I do buy too much. Make a list and stick to it, if you can. But if I see some extraordinary produce not on my list such as fresh shelling beans, like cranberry or flageolet, I can't resist. They go into my canvas market bag. Keeping in mind that produce is perishable, I only buy what I can eat in the next few days. The hardest part of shopping at the farmer's market is knowing when to stop.

To find your local farmer's market, try contacting your state department of agriculture or local, county cooperative extension office or www.localharvest.org.

Grilled Ratatouille

Serves 4-6

If you like regular ratatouille, then you will really like this. The vegetables have a terrific smoky flavor and distinctly more intact texture. Grilling gives new meaning to this dish.

2	**red peppers**
1	**yellow or orange pepper**
2	**heads garlic**
3	**tablespoons olive oil**
1	**medium red onion, cut into chunks**
2	**medium eggplant or 6 Japanese eggplant, cut into slices 1/2-inch thick**
2	**medium zucchini, cut into 1-2-inch chunks**
2	**yellow squash, cut into 1-2-inch chunks**
8	**roma tomatoes or 3 ripe tomatoes**
1	**teaspoon coriander seeds, crushed lightly**
1	**tablespoon chopped capers**
1/2	**cup fresh basil, chopped fine**
1/4	**cup Italian parsley, chopped fine**
1	**tablespoon fresh oregano leaves, chopped fine**
5	**cloves garlic, minced**
2	**tablespoons balsamic vinegar**
1/4	**cup extra virgin olive oil**

Salt and freshly ground pepper, to taste

Place the red and yellow peppers directly over the flame and grill until charred on all sides. Put into a bowl and cover or into a paper or plastic bag and let steam for 10 minutes. Remove blackened skin and seeds and cut into chunks. Set aside in a bowl, saving all juices.

Coat the two heads of garlic with a bit of the 3 tablespoons of olive oil. Wrap in foil and place on the grill. Let cook for 20 to 30 minutes, or more, until the garlic is soft. Let cool and remove the softened cloves. Set aside with the peppers.

Brush the eggplant, zucchini, yellow squash and tomatoes with olive oil. Place the eggplant on the grill and grill for 5 minutes on each side, until soft. Place the remaining vegetables on a rack on the grill and cook 3 minutes, cut side down and then flip.

When all the vegetables are cooked, cut into pieces approximately the same size. Combine and add the crushed coriander seeds, capers, basil, parsley, oregano, garlic, vinegar and olive oil. Add salt and pepper, to taste.

Roasted Vegetable Fajitas

Serves 4-6

*W*hen the weather is too hot to use the oven, put all the veggies on the grill. Either way, almost everyone likes this tempting dish. Serve lots of warm corn tortillas on the side. And for me, mucho cilantro.

3	**red peppers, cut in half**
1	**jalapeno pepper**
1	**Anaheim pepper, cut in half**
1	**large onion, sliced**
1	**head garlic, cloves separated but not peeled**
1	**tablespoon olive oil**
4	**medium tomatoes**
1	**tablespoon chili powder**
2	**teaspoons Mexican seasoning**

Dash of cayenne, to taste
Juice of 1 lime
6-12 Corn or flour tortillas
Salsa (optional)

Preheat oven to 500° F.

Combine the peppers, onion, garlic with the oil and spices and spread on a parchment-lined baking sheet. Add the tomatoes and place the baking sheet in the hot oven. Cook for 30 to 40 minutes, until everything is well cooked. Remove the peppers and place in a bowl, covered with plastic. Remove the skins, ribs and seeds. Cut the large peppers into strips. Mince the jalapeno. Peel the garlic cloves. Cut the tomatoes into quarters. Combine all the vegetables with the lime juice. Serve in warm tortillas with salsa, if desired.

Seitan Sauté

Serves 4

*S*eitan is wheat gluten. My students either love it or hate it. It is a meat substitute that has a chewy texture. You can make it or buy it already prepared in a "beef" or "chicken" style. If you don't like it, substitute tofu, tempeh or neither. It will still be delicious.

1	**tablespoon canola or rice bran oil**
1	**medium onion, sliced**
1	**pound of seitan, marinated in tamari broth, cut in small chunks**
1/2	**pound mushrooms, sliced**
2	**cloves garlic, minced**
1	**teaspoon grated ginger**
1/2	**cup pineapple juice**
2	**tablespoons rice vinegar**
1	**tablespoon seitan marinade or reduced sodium tamari**
1	**cup snow or sugar snap peas, trimmed**
1	**tablespoon arrowroot mixed with 1 tablespoon water**

Heat oil in large sauté pan. Add onion and cook for about 5 minutes until it starts getting translucent. Add seitan, mushrooms, garlic and ginger and sauté for about 3 minutes. Add the pineapple juice, vinegar and marinade. Stir. Add the snow peas. Cook until the snow peas are almost cooked. Remove pan from heat and add the arrowroot mixture to the pan. Stir quickly to incorporate. Put back on heat and heat through.

Serve hot over rice, quinoa, another grain or noodles.

Pasta with Tempeh-Corn Sauce

Serves 4

*T*empeh is a fermented soy cake used often in Indonesia, and a less processed product than tofu. It has not gained a lot of acceptance in this country although I've been trying for 20 years now. Maybe you'll like it.

1/2	cup garlic or other broth
1	clove garlic, minced
2	teaspoons tamari
1	small hot pepper, minced (optional)
1	teaspoon crushed coriander seeds (optional)
8	ounces tempeh, cubed
2	large or 3 small ears corn

Vegetable cooking spray

1/2	onion, diced
2	tablespoons arrowroot
3	roma tomatoes, peeled and chopped
	or 1/2 pint cherry tomatoes, diced

Salt and pepper to taste
8 to 12 ounces pasta, cooked al dente

Combine garlic broth, garlic, tamari, pepper and coriander seeds. Marinate tempeh in this mixture for about 10 to 15 minutes.

Cut corn kernels off cob and set aside.

Spray a medium skillet with cooking spray. Sauté onion over medium heat. Add corn kernels and cook for about 5 minutes or until onion begins to turn translucent. Drain tempeh from marinade, reserving marinade. Add tempeh to pan, adding a little marinade if tempeh begins to stick. Cook for 1 to 2 minutes until tempeh begins to brown.

Mix arrowroot with marinade.

Add tomatoes to tempeh mixture and cook until tomatoes begin to break down slightly.

Remove pan from the heat. Whisk arrowroot-marinade and stir into tempeh mixture. Put back on heat and cook until the sauce turns glossy and thick. Season with salt and pepper. Pour over hot pasta.

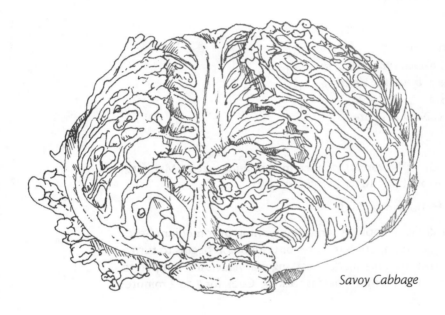

Savoy Cabbage

"No cook who has attained mastery over her craft ever apologizes for the presence of garlic in her productions."

Ruth Gottfried,
The Questing Cook (1927)

Fall

*J*ust when I'd thought that it wasn't possible to be excited about the change of seasons since summer is my favorite, I become enchanted with fall. Where I live in California, autumn is the time of true abundance and harvest. The grapes are getting picked, yet the tomatoes, corn, eggplant and the first of the winter squash are too. In early autumn my creative cooking juices flow even more so than in summer. The heat dissipates, the nights cool down and there are abundant vegetable choices. Salads are still appealing, though the ingredients are heartier.

As the last of the tomatoes appear at the market, I don't even think about buying them; I am already weaning myself, waiting for next summer's crop to arrive. I say "so long" to all the summer vegetables and welcome what the fall has to offer – roots, tubers and hard squash. Gnarly, fat celery root appears. Winter squash, including my favorite, delicata, shows up. Then a new variety or two begs me to buy and try. This past year it was the bright orange Sunshine that caught my eye and palate. Farmer Neil Dunaetz of EasySweet Farm in Santa Rosa says that he thinks that this will become the prototypical winter squash soon. I hope that he is right for it is superior to butternut or acorn – the two supermarket standbys. Vow to try a new squash this year. You may be glad that you did. I was.

Stuffed Shiitake Mushrooms

Serves 4-8 as an appetizer

*A*ppetizers don't need to be complicated. This one works because everyone knows that it is a treat to have shiitake mushrooms. You can boost your immune system while savoring the flavors.

Vegetable oil spray (optional)
1   medium onion, chopped
1   clove garlic, minced
2   tablespoons chopped fresh Italian parsley
4   ounces sausage flavor Gimme Lean or other soy sausage
1/2   cup breadcrumbs
8 to 12 large shiitake mushrooms

Preheat the oven to 350° F.

Spray a small bit of oil in a large sauté pan placed over medium heat. Add the onion and sauté until it turns translucent, about 5 minutes. Add the garlic and sauté another minute. If the mixture begins to stick, add a tablespoon of water or broth.

Put the cooked onions and garlic into a bowl. Add the parsley, Gimme Lean and bread crumbs and stir to combine.

Cut the stems away from the mushrooms as they are quite tough (but you can save them for stock). Mound the filling into the mushroom caps with a spoon, pressing firmly with the inside of the spoon to form a smooth mound. Put the mushrooms on a baking sheet. Bake for 15 to 20 minutes or until the filling feels firm and hot. These must be served hot or the filling texture will be mushy.

Note: To make breadcrumbs, you can use fresh, stale or lightly toasted bread. Put one slice into the food processor and process until you have crumbs.

Dry Sautéing

Some authors of fat-free recipes suggest adding some type of liquid to pan "sauté" the initial ingredients, which for me usually includes onions and garlic. But what you end up with are steamed or boiled vegetables instead of a sauté.

My technique requires that you have a heavy-bottomed nonstick pan. Most of these pans should not be used over heat higher than medium as it tends to burn the pan's nonstick coating. That's why I start with a dry pan over medium heat.

I call this technique dry sautéing. Put the pan on medium heat for a few minutes. Add the ingredients in the order listed and for the recommended cooking times. The key to preventing burnt food is to stir occasionally and look at the ingredients to be sure nothing is sticking or burning. If that begins to happen, add water, broth, juice or wine, a tablespoon at a time so you can easily scrape off the stuck-on food particles. Do not add so much liquid that the ingredients get soggy, or you will not be sautéing.

I have found that dry sautéing is the best oil-free method for extracting the most flavor from food. It is one of the easiest ways I know of for eliminating a tablespoon of fat and 100 calories from your diet.

Szechwan Eggplant Roll-Ups

Makes 16-20

*Y*ou can freeze the grilled eggplant. When you defrost it you'll continue the recipe by making the filling and rolling up the eggplant. You could also bake the eggplant slices or grill them on a stovetop grill, if you had to, but cooking over fire makes them taste best. In this case, salting the eggplant makes it more pliable. Be careful not to over-salt or they will be salty.

2-3 medium to large eggplants
  totaling 1 1/2-2 pounds
Salt

Marinade:

Makes 1/3 cup

1 tablespoon canola oil
1 tablespoon toasted sesame oil
1 tablespoon tamari
3 tablespoons rice vinegar
1 tablespoon grated ginger
1 clove garlic, crushed
1 green onion, sliced fine

Mix all together.
The marinade may be stored for a few days.

Filling:

1 tablespoon canola oil
1 cup sliced green onion
1 tablespoon grated ginger
2 cloves garlic, minced
1 teaspoon chili paste with garlic
1 roasted red or Anaheim pepper, diced small
1 tablespoon tamari or 3/4 teaspoon salt
1 package Mori Nu firm tofu, blended

Sauté the green onion, ginger and garlic in the canola oil for 5 minutes. Add the chili paste, roasted pepper and tamari or salt. Blend with the tofu. Use to stuff eggplant.

Slice the eggplant lengthwise into slices 1/4 to 1/3 of an inch and no thicker. Salt lightly on both sides and let stand 30 minutes to an hour. Rinse off the salt and blot dry. Place the eggplant slices in the marinade in a zippered plastic bag or glass baking dish. Let marinate for at least 15 minutes. Remove from the marinade and grill for 2-3 minutes on each side until cooked through and flexible but not blackened. Or bake in the oven at 400° F. for 3 to 4 minutes on each side. Remove them from the grill or oven and stack them together on a plate for at least 5 minutes. They will soften even more.

When the eggplant is softened, hold it lengthwise in front of you. Put a tablespoon or so of filling about 1 inch from the bottom of the slice. Roll upwards until tight. Put seam side down for final baking. If the rolls seem like they are falling apart, use toothpicks to hold them together.

Bake eggplant at 350° for 5-10 minutes, until heated through. Serve hot or warm, garnished with roasted red pepper.

Curried White and Sweet Potato Pancakes with Fresh Fruit Chutney

Makes about 20-30 small pancakes

*T*his variation on traditional potato pancakes makes them even tastier. Grating the potatoes in the food processor makes the recipe faster to prepare.

1 1/2 pounds large potatoes, like russets or Yukon golds, grated
1 1/2 pounds sweet potatoes or garnet yams, grated
1   large onion, grated
1   tablespoon egg replacer mixed with 1/4 cup water or 1 egg and 2 egg whites, beaten
1/4   cup all purpose or whole wheat pastry flour
1   teaspoon baking powder
1/2   teaspoon salt
1   tablespoon curry powder
2   tablespoons canola oil

Mix the potato, sweet potato and onion together well in a large bowl. Squeeze out any excess liquid and drain. Add the egg replacer mixture, flour, baking powder, salt and curry powder and mix well.

Add 1 tablespoon of oil to a large nonstick skillet over medium heat.

Place 1/4 cup batter for each pancake into the skillet. Cover with a lid until the bottoms are golden brown, about 5 minutes. Flip to the other side and cook until golden brown. Serve hot with chutney. If the pancakes are done and there are still more to cook, which there will be, then put them on a baking sheet in a 300 ˚ oven to keep warm.

Fresh Fruit Chutney with Mustard Seeds and Cilantro

Makes about 1 cup

Juice of 1 lime
1   apple, unpeeled and diced
1/4   cup minced red onion
1   tablespoon maple syrup
1   tablespoon raspberry vinegar
1   tablespoon black mustard seeds, toasted
2   tablespoons chopped fresh cilantro

Squeeze the lime juice over the diced apple. Combine with the rest of the ingredients and let sit for at least 15 minutes before serving.

Note: *if you want this chutney to be hot, mince a half a jalapeno or hotter pepper and add it.*

Lemon Scented Spinach Spread

Makes 1 1/2 cups

*T*his is a tasty way to get people to eat more vegetables. It is far healthier than the spinach dip that many have gotten used to. You can use this to make wrap sandwiches as well as putting it in a traditional "bread bowl."

1	10 ounce package frozen chopped spinach, thawed, drained and squeezed dry
1/2	cup chopped green onions
1/2	package Mori Nu silken lite tofu
1/4	cup fresh lemon juice, to taste
1	teaspoon lemon zest (be sure to zest before juicing)
2	teaspoons Dijon mustard
1-2	teaspoons Sucanat or sugar, to taste

Salt and pepper, to taste
Lemon zest and lemon slices for garnish

Combine the spinach and green onions in the food processor and pulse. Add the tofu, lemon juice and zest, and mustard. Process until smooth. Add salt, pepper, lemon juice and Sucanat, to taste. Serve immediately after making it or make a day ahead and serve chilled. If you make it ahead be sure to taste before serving as sometimes the flavors get muted. Garnish with twisted lemon slices and lemon zest strips.

Polenta Triangles with Roasted Red Pepper Relish

Makes enough for 8-10 people as an appetizer

I have made this recipe for many years, always to rave reviews. You have to plan to make the polenta in advance since it needs to cool and set up.

I've made the relish without the polenta but I think that they taste great together. If you end up with extra red peppers in the jar, you may want to wrap them in plastic and store them in the freezer for later use.

1 1/4 cups coarsely ground cornmeal
3 1/2 cups water
1   teaspoon salt

Boil water. Stir in cornmeal. Turn down heat and continue to stir cornmeal so that it doesn't stick. Cook, stirring constantly, for 5 to 10 minutes or until a spoon will stand straight up in the cornmeal mixture. Pour this into a baking sheet and make it into a thin layer. Refrigerate for 15 to 20 minutes or until cooled. Cut into triangles (or your favorite shape) and place on a plate. Serve at room temperature topped with the relish.

Note: *You may also add fresh chopped herbs, such as basil, parsley, thyme or oregano when making polenta.*

Relish:

1   10-ounce jar roasted red peppers or
**   2 large red peppers, roasted**
2   tablespoons capers, chopped
1   tablespoon chopped fresh Italian parsley
1   tablespoon chopped fresh basil
1   clove garlic, pressed
1   tablespoon extra virgin olive oil
2   teaspoons balsamic vinegar

Finely chop roasted red peppers. (You may do this in a food processor.) Combine with the remaining ingredients. Let this mixture sit at room temperature for at least 30 minutes so that the flavors can meld. Serve on top of polenta or on the side.

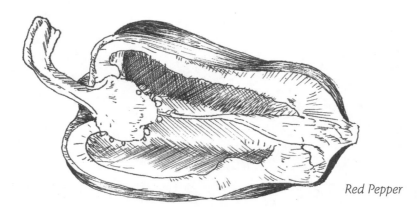

Red Pepper

Baked Sweet Potato Rounds with Cranberry Orange Relish

Each potato makes approximately 25 rounds. Use these as the base for the cranberry relish.

Line a baking sheet with parchment paper, or, if you must, aluminum foil. Peel the sweet potatoes and cut into thin slices, either by hand with a sharp knife or by using the slicing blade of your food processor.

Preheat the oven to 350° F.

Arrange the slices so that they don't touch. Bake for 15 minutes. Remove from oven, turn slices and bake another 5 minutes. Serve hot, warm or let cool and reheat a bit before serving.

Top with cranberry relish, cranberry chutney or your favorite topper.

Fresh Cranberry Orange Relish
Makes 2 cups

This is what I like to eat at Thanksgiving. It's so much tastier than the stuff in the can.

1	organic orange, unpeeled
1	cup cranberries, fresh or frozen and thawed
2-3	tablespoons (or more) maple syrup, Sucanat or sugar
1	medium ripe pear, cored

Wash orange well and cut into quarters.

Combine cranberries, orange, pear and maple syrup in food processor. Process until mixture is still chunky. If not sweet enough for you, add more maple syrup.

Make ahead and serve chilled or at room temperature.

Lentil, Mushroom and Walnut Pate

Serves 8-10 as an appetizer

Be liberal with your use of parsley, as this dish does not have brilliant colors despite its lively taste.

1	cup dried green lentils
1/2	ounce dried wild mushrooms
2	medium leeks, white part only, chopped
1/2	pound crimini mushrooms, thinly sliced
2	large garlic cloves, minced
1	clove garlic, crushed
1/2	cup finely chopped toasted walnuts plus 1/4 cup toasted halves for topping
1	tablespoon chopped fresh thyme or 2 tablespoons dried thyme
4	tablespoons quick-cooking or baby oats or oat flour

Salt and freshly ground pepper

1/4	teaspoon paprika
2	tablespoons balsamic vinegar
4	tablespoons chopped Italian parsley

Pick over the lentils and put them in a pot. Cover with water and let them cook until they are soft, 35 to 45 minutes. Drain, reserving liquid, and set aside.

Pour boiling water over the dried wild mushrooms and let them soak for 15 to 30 minutes.

Heat the medium skillet. Add the leeks and dry sauté for 2 to 3 minutes. Squeeze the water out of the wild mushrooms (saving the water) and add the mushrooms to the pan along with the crimini mushrooms, minced garlic and 1/2 cup walnuts. Cook over medium heat until the mushrooms release their liquid, about 10 to 13 minutes. Add the thyme and oats and cook for 4 to 5 minutes longer.

Puree mushroom mixture in the food processor with the lentils and vinegar, adding 1/4 teaspoon freshly ground pepper and 1/4 teaspoon paprika. If the mixture seems too thick, add some lentil cooking liquid or mushroom soaking liquid. Taste and add salt, if necessary.

Line a 3 to 4 cup terrine or narrow 10 X 4-inch bread pan with parchment or wax paper. Sprinkle the parsley and 1/4 cup walnuts over the paper and add the lentil-mushroom mixture. Cover and refrigerate for at least 30 minutes until cooled down.

When ready to serve, unmold the pate by pulling at the paper lining to ease the pate from the sides of the pan. Set a platter over the pate and then invert. Ease the pan off the pate, then peel off the paper. Surround the pate with sprigs of parsley and cherry tomatoes, if in season.

Serve at room temperature with crackers or bread or Crostini (see page 90).

Pear and Toasted Walnut Salad with Cranberry Vinaigrette

Serves 4 to 6

*T*his salad has flavors that speak fall to me — pears, walnuts, bitter greens and cranberries. You can substitute other dried fruit if you like. Be sure to have really ripe pears. This usually means buying them a few days before you need them.

1/2	cup water or vegetable broth
1	tablespoon cornstarch
1/4	cup orange juice
2	tablespoons balsamic vinegar
1	teaspoon Dijon mustard
1/4	cup dried cranberries
3	tablespoons walnut halves or pieces, toasted
2	large ripe pears, each cut into 8 to 12 slices
4 to 6 cups greens, including bitter ones like arugula or cress	
Freshly ground pepper, to taste	

Combine water and cornstarch in a small saucepan. Bring almost to the boil, until thickened, about 5 minutes. Remove from heat and let cool.

Combine the above mixture with the orange juice, balsamic vinegar, mustard and 2 tablespoons of the cranberries in a food processor. Set aside.

Put washed and dried greens in a large bowl. Arrange pears over greens and sprinkle walnuts and cranberries over pears. Add dressing and toss. Top with freshly ground pepper. Serve right away.

Vegetable Enthusiasts

Vegetables can be fun, interesting and inspirational. I want you to get as enthused about vegetables as I do. I look forward to my weekly forays to the farmer's market. In the winter I have two opportunities every week. In the summer, many more.

Paula Downing, farmer's market manager in Santa Rosa and Sebastopol (CA), recently referred to me as a "die-hard" shopper.

To that I replied, "I have to eat all year round. At least here I know what's in season." In supermarkets or other food stores, it's hard to tell that tomatoes or zucchini aren't in season in January. I see them in the advertisements, called "market fresh" produce. I am sure that they are fresh from some market but not mine and most likely not grown within this country.

At the farmer's market I can purchase varieties of vegetables that I don't see at stores because perhaps they are oddly shaped or don't ship well. I have relationships with the people that grow my food or their employees. They may not all know my name but they recognize me because I have been a steadfast customer. Sometimes the farmer offers me a bonus enticement of a vegetable that I've never before tried, hoping that I will spread the word and become a convert myself. Often it works.

Face it, most of us are at least a little reluctant to try new things, especially those that are green (as many vegetables are). My motto is, "I'll try anything once. If I like it, I'll try it again." I have written this book for those of you who are not as brave as I am so that you will have someone you can trust to lead you through the wonderful world of vegetables. Please become part of my "queendom", also known as the vegetable kingdom, where there are many treasures and jewels to discover. Lettuce begin.

Giving Thanks

In terms of eating seasonally I wonder why Thanksgiving is in late November. Shouldn't it be the third week of October? Of course I understand the whole story with the Pilgrims and the Indians (now known as Native Americans) and why it was a celebration. Yet I want to celebrate in October, for that is when so many of the vegetables that I love are in season.

My mind spins thinking about the holiday meal that I could create with corn, peppers, eggplant, tomatoes, summer and winter squash and green beans, to name just some of what is available. Local produce dwindles after late October with the change to cooler, cloudy and rainy weather. The offerings are still vibrant and tasty but how can one compare celery root or cabbage with a ripe tomato or deep red pimiento pepper?

Perhaps all those hundreds of years ago, long before the refrigerator and grocery store, finding something to eat was reason enough to give thanks. Now it seems that Thanksgiving is just another meal, one that often does not reflect seasonal foods. I give thanks for all the food in every season.

The vibrancy of food is evident when it's at the peak of freshness. Asparagus is best when it pops up in the spring and summer's reflection is seen in a vine-ripe tomato. (Try that with a store-bought tomato in January.)

The cooler months bring fall and winter ingredients such as pomegranates and their seeds, fuyu persimmons, pineapple guavas, cranberries, almonds and more that I combine to make into a colorful, flavor-packed salad.

Bright Autumn Salad

Serves 4

*M*ost of these ingredients are native to my area of Northern California. If you cannot find them, substitute the most colorful and freshest seasonal fruit. You are aiming for a colorful salad that is sweet, tart, crunchy and bitter. I imagine that the Native Americans living where I do would have served this for their Thanksgiving meal (held in October, of course) using local, wild bitter greens instead of endive or radicchio.

1	**medium head radicchio or 3 small heads of Belgian endive, sliced into shreds**
2	**fuyu (firm, flat Asian) persimmons, seeded if necessary, and diced**
1/2	**pomegranate, cut, arils (seeds) removed to be used**
3-4	**pineapple guava (feijoa), if available, or kiwi, peeled and diced**
1/4	**cup or more dried cranberries**
1/4	**cup toasted slivered or sliced almonds**
1-2	**tablespoons raspberry or other fruit vinegar (optional)**

Cut the bitter greens or reds into shreds. Put on a plate.

In a medium bowl, combine the persimmons, pomegranate, pineapple guava, and most of the cranberries and almonds. Arrange the combined mixture over the shredded bitter greens. Top with the remaining cranberries and almonds. Drizzle fruit vinegar over the top, if desired.

Thai-inspired Broccoli Slaw

Serves 4

I love plain steamed broccoli but this elevates broccoli to new heights. If you want this to be a main meal salad, add some baked tofu or seitan cubes.

Freeze the remaining coconut milk in ice cube or other small amounts so that you won't have to open a can every time you need coconut milk. It will last about 3 months in the freezer.

1	**large bunch broccoli, about 2 pounds**
1	**tablespoon finely chopped fresh lemongrass**
1	**kaffir lime leaf, if available or 1 teaspoon lime zest and 1/2 teaspoon juice**
1/4	**cup boiling water or stock**
1/4	**cup peanut butter**
1	**tablespoon rice vinegar**
1	**teaspoon grated ginger**
1	**clove garlic, crushed**
1/4	**teaspoon crushed red pepper flakes**
1/4	**cup lite or regular coconut milk**
1	**tablespoon Bragg's liquid amino acids or tamari**
1-2	**tablespoons lime juice**
Sweetener to taste	
2	**tablespoons finely chopped roasted red pepper**
1/4	**cup minced fresh cilantro**
2	**tablespoons finely chopped green onions**

Cut the broccoli into small florets. Peel the stalks and cut them into slices 1/2-inch thick. Steam over boiling water for 3 to 5 minutes until tender. Remove from heat and put into a bowl. Refrigerate to cool until ready.

Pour the boiling water over the lemongrass and kaffir lime leaf in a heatproof bowl. Let sit for at least 10 minutes to extract flavor.

Strain the lemongrass water and put into a blender. Combine with the remaining ingredients except the cilantro and green onions. Blend until smooth. Taste and adjust the seasonings.

Pour dressing over the broccoli. Add the roasted red pepper and toss. Garnish with the cilantro and green onions. This tastes great right away but sometimes tastes even better the next day, if any is left over.

Hot and Smoky Potato Salad
with Chipotle Peppers

Serves 4-6

*T*his potato salad is a definite twist on a traditional version. I have yet to find a vegetarian potato salad that I haven't liked. If you didn't want to make your own dressing, combine your favorite mayonnaise with ground chipotle pepper or chipotle powder and garlic.

2	pounds potatoes, such as small red, **Yellow Finn or Yukon Gold**
1/2	cup chopped celery
1/2	cup red onion, finely chopped

Dressing:

2	tablespoons mellow white miso
1/2	package Mori Nu firm lite silken tofu
2	tablespoons white wine vinegar or other light colored vinegar
1	clove garlic, crushed
1/2-1	chipotle pepper, seeds removed and chopped, rehydrated
1	teaspoon honey or other sweetener
1/2	teaspoon salt or 1 teaspoon tamari

Vegetable broth or water, as needed
Salt and pepper, to taste

1/4	cup chopped cilantro or Italian parsley

Cut potatoes in half lengthwise. Then cut them into 1 1/2-inch pieces. Place in a steamer over boiling water. Steam for 10 to 15 minutes until a knife easily goes through the potatoes. When done set aside.

While the potatoes are cooking, combine the dressing ingredients, miso through vegetable broth in a blender. Blend well until smooth. Taste and adjust seasonings. Add salt and pepper to taste.

Put the potatoes, celery and onion in a large bowl. Pour the dressing over the warm potato pieces. Stir to combine. Garnish with the cilantro or stir it in, depending on how much you like cilantro. If you don't, use parsley instead. Serve warm.

Tierra Vegetables:
The "Cheers" of Farm Stands

That's what Evie Truxaw told me she calls the farmstand that she runs with her farmer husband Wayne James (who learned about going barefoot in the Peace Corps) and his sister Lee. Evie wants to know all the shoppers and have them interact with one another. And darn, it seems to be working.

Almost every time that I've been there recently, which is only open Tuesdays and Fridays in the winter, I have met someone new. Now I know their names.

"The farmstand is even better than what I had hoped for," says Evie, grinning with excitement. I am certain Evie's enduring energy has contributed to the farm's vibrant health. The sustainable growing practices employed by Wayne and Lee are also critical. They have turned a barren 17-acre parcel of Sonoma County Open Space land bordering Highway 101, just north of Santa Rosa, into a thriving vegetable oasis.

Tierra Vegetables is best known for their peppers, chiles, fresh and dried, chipotle (smoked) chiles and chile jam. While I love those products, the biggest draw for me is fresh tree collards, Jerusalem artichokes, orange cauliflower that has just been picked that morning, or even at my request. (Wayne will stride barefoot out into the field and get something if you ask nicely and with enthusiasm.)

When I stop by the stand I feel like a kid in a candy store, so to speak. I almost always buy more than I need and then find creative uses for my purchases.

Do you know anyone that needs a 5-pound Lutz variety beet? I got a number of great, sweet dishes from that one. I even froze beets for the first time. Some days the dinosaur kale beckons me. Other times I am inspired by the Italian puntarella greens, a head of Savoy cabbage or enticing escarole. But in the winter the main reason I go is to buy the sweetest imaginable carrots that I lovingly cut up daily as an integral part of my husband Rick's lunch.

Since we need to eat year round, I suggest that you find a farm or two, and support them in their endeavors. Without the people that grow our food, how will we survive?

Garlic

Roasted Red Pepper and Tomato Soup

Serves 6-8

*T*omatoes and red peppers signal summer and early fall like no other veggies. I love the intense flavors of both. This soup combines them well, and can be served hot, or chilled as the base for gazpacho.

1	**tablespoon olive oil**
1	**large sweet onion, diced**
6	**cloves garlic, minced**
2	**teaspoons ground cumin**
3	**pounds beefsteak or heirloom tomatoes, cored and cut into chunks**
2	**large red bell peppers, roasted, seeded and cut into eighths**
2	**large bay leaves**
1/4	**teaspoon saffron threads**

Salt to taste
Freshly ground black pepper, to taste

1/4	**cup chopped fresh parsley**
1/4	**cup chopped fresh basil**
2	**tablespoons sherry or red wine vinegar, for garnish**

Heat the oil in a large soup pot. Add the onion and sauté on medium heat for about 5 minutes, until it starts turning translucent. Add the garlic and cumin. Sauté for another couple of minutes. Add the tomatoes, peppers, bay leaves, saffron and salt.

Bring to a boil, then reduce the heat to a simmer. Simmer for 20 to 30 minutes, until the tomatoes are thoroughly broken down. Remove the bay leaves. Put the soup through a food mill for the smoothest texture. If you don't have one use a hand blender or a food processor to puree the soup, and leave it as is or pass it through a sieve. Taste and adjust salt and pepper. Stir in the parsley and basil. Finish with a splash of sherry vinegar.

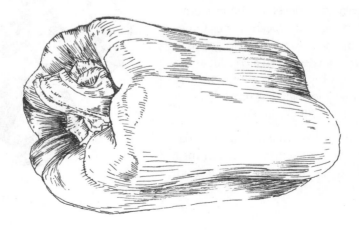

The Veggie Queen™: Vegetables Get The Royal Treatment

Red Peppers

Roasted Pepper Reflections

This year I didn't roast any red or yellow peppers to store in my freezer. Larry, the organic farmer who grew my favorite peppers, apples and more on the ranch that had been in his family for decades, sold the farm and moved to Washington State with his wife. He worked hard. My guess is that the proceeds from selling the farm afforded him the opportunity for living a nice, quiet life somewhere else. But this leaves me without his peppers, and wondering about the future of our local farms.

When Julia, a food colleague, told me late in the spring that Larry wouldn't be at the farmer's market anymore, I told her that she had ruined my day. In the summer other growers had peppers but none seemed of the same quality and quantity. They were more expensive and didn't appear as pampered. I missed my chance but organic roasted red peppers are available in a jar, so all is not lost.

I have so enjoyed being able to reach into the freezer and open a zippered plastic bag filled with my home-roasted peppers neatly plastic-wrapped in single pepper bundles. They were easy to defrost and perfect for most recipes that call for roasted pepper as a garnish or accent. Now, I need another plan, having missed my annual day-long pepper roasting ritual.

Maybe next year I will realize that if I want to find those roasted peppers in my freezer, someone else will be getting my pepper business. I hope that Larry is happily lazing in his lounge chair in Washington.

Harvest Vegetable Soup

Serves 6-8

*U*se whatever vegetables are harvest fresh for this soup. If you have corn or green beans, add them when you add the tomato.

2	tablespoons canola oil
2	medium leeks, sliced
5	cloves garlic, minced
3	cups peeled, cubed winter squash like Delicata, Sweet Dumpling or Butternut
3	cups sliced potatoes, like Yukon Gold
1/2	cup diced carrot
6	cups Allium Broth
1	sweet red pepper, diced
2	large tomatoes (heirloom if possible), peeled, seeded and chopped
	Salt and pepper, to taste
3	tablespoons chopped basil plus basil for garnish

Add the canola oil to a soup pot. Add the leeks and sauté over medium heat for about 5 minutes. Add the garlic and sauté for 5 more minutes, being careful not to burn the garlic. Add the squash, potatoes, carrot and the broth. Bring the mixture to a boil, then reduce to a simmer. Simmer for 20 minutes or until the squash and potatoes are soft. Puree the squash-potato mixture with a hand blender, or in the blender or food processor in batches until smooth. Return to the soup pot, if using blender or processor. Return to a simmer and add the chopped red pepper, tomato and basil. Simmer until tomatoes are broken down and pepper is softened, about 10 to 15 minutes. Add salt and pepper, to taste. Garnish with basil.

Allium Broth

Makes 7- 8 cups

The basis for Harvest Vegetable Soup is Allium Broth, which works well in many other soups too.

	Vegetable oil spray
2	tablespoons minced garlic (1 large or 2 small heads)
1	medium onion, chopped
1	leek, cleaned well and sliced
8	cups water
1	sprig fresh sage or 1/2 teaspoon dried sage
3	sprigs Italian parsley
1	sprig fresh thyme
	Salt and ground black pepper, to taste

Spray a pot with oil. Add the onion, garlic and leek and cook until the onion is transparent. Add the water and herbs and bring the mixture to a boil. Reduce the heat to a simmer. Simmer covered for 15 to 30 minutes.

Strain. Season with salt and pepper.

This will keep in the refrigerator for 1 week and it freezes well.

Donna's Meal

My sister Donna attends the farmer's market on the opposite coast of the U.S. once a week like I do. Since she lives in Maryland and the time is 3 hours earlier, I can call her on Sunday morning at 9 a.m. to find out what she bought at the market just as I am about to head to my farmer's market, shopping bag in tow. During parts of October and November similar produce is available at both markets. Earlier in the year Donna's local tomatoes are in season far ahead of mine. But no matter, for shopping at the farmer's market keeps one in tune with what is local and seasonal.

Donna and I have a similar cooking style, which is to first look in the refrigerator and see what is there. Donna called and told me that she laughed at herself yesterday, after doing a refrigerator sweep. "When I first looked I thought I didn't have anything to eat but then I realized that I did," she said.

Donna thought that the meal she prepared was so tasty, she actually wrote it down. (This is rare and remarkable, since she once taught a small cooking class for inexperienced cooks. A few hours before the class she called and asked, "Do you think that the students need a written recipe?" After a brief pause I answered, "Of course they do.")

"It took 45 minutes from the start until I was drinking a glass of wine and eating! And I did it all in one pan," she boasted.

Here's Donna's meal

Start by cooking some medium grain brown rice in the rice cooker. (I would do it in the pressure cooker at high pressure for 22 minutes with a natural pressure release.) When cooked, add the pine nuts that have been dry toasted in the pan below.

Sautéed Asian greens with garlic

Add a bit of olive oil to a pan over medium heat. When it gets hot add a few cloves of minced garlic and sauté the greens until they are bright green. Add a little sea salt and pepper. Set these aside to keep warm.

Diced onions, parsnips, carrots and apple with sweet and spicy sauce on sautéed red cabbage

Add a bit of olive oil to a pan over medium heat. Add 1 cup chopped onion, 1 sliced parsnip and 1 sliced carrot. Cook until the vegetables are just cooked through. Add a tablespoon of orange marmalade, 1 teaspoon of chopped jalapeno or serano chile and a tablespoon or two of water, wine or broth. Let that cook for another minute and then add 1 small chopped apple. Sprinkle on sea salt and remove the mixture from the pan.

Add 2 cups finely sliced red cabbage to the pan and cook until it is wilted, about 5 minutes. Put the red cabbage on a plate and arrange the cooked vegetables on top.

Lemony Kohlrabi on chopped tatsoi

Chop a couple of handfuls of tatsoi. Grate the kohlrabi, add 1 tablespoon of lemon juice, a couple of teaspoons olive oil and salt and pepper. Serve the kohlrabi like salad on top of the tatsoi.

Put all these dishes on a large platter, and enjoy.

Donna's final comment: *"The whole thing was fabulous - which is why I don't eat out more!"*

Herb Roasted Root Vegetables

Serves 4

*T*his is a satisfying and really easy dish to make. The aroma fills the house and makes guests hungry for the meal. I make it whenever I want substantial leftovers. Use any root vegetables that you like such as rutabagas, leeks, shallots. Only use white or gold beets, if they are available. Red ones will color your entire dish of vegetables. If you are following the McDougall program you can make this recipe using a couple of tablespoons of broth instead of the oil.

2	onions, cut into halves or quarters
10	cloves garlic, unpeeled
2	cups carrots, peeled and cut into 1 to 2-inch pieces
1	medium celery root, peeled, cut into 1 to 2-inch pieces
2	parsnips, peeled and cut into 1-inch pieces
3	small turnips, peeled and cut in half to about 2-inch pieces
1-2	Japanese or regular sweet potatoes (not yams), peeled and cut into 3-inch pieces
1	cup winter squash, peeled and cut into 2-inch cubes
2-3	potatoes, cut into quarters, about 2-inches
1-2	white or gold beets, peeled and cut into quarters (optional)
2	tablespoons olive oil

Salt and pepper

3	sprigs rosemary
3	sprigs thyme

Preheat the oven to 425° F.

Combine all the vegetables in a large glass baking dish. Add the olive oil, salt and pepper and toss well. Add the herb sprigs. Cover the dish. Bake for 40 minutes. Remove the cover and see if the vegetables are cooked through. Cook for another 5 minutes or until the vegetables are tender but not mushy. Serve hot.

Greens Braised with Tomatoes and Thyme

Serves 4

I am always looking for new ways to cook greens to make them tasty and interesting. It seems almost impossible to eat too many of them.

6   cups chopped greens, such as kale, turnip or collards
1 1/2 cups peeled, seeded, chopped fresh or
       canned, diced tomatoes
1/2   cup red wine
1   teaspoon sugar
1   tablespoon vegetable bouillon powder
3   cloves garlic, minced
1-2   sprigs fresh thyme
1   cinnamon stick
2   tablespoons fruity olive oil

Combine all ingredients in a nonreactive saucepan and simmer covered for 30 minutes. Uncover and cook another 15 minutes, or longer to reduce slightly if you prefer a thicker sauce. Remove the cinnamon stick and thyme stems. Serve as a side dish or over noodles, quinoa or other grain.

Simple Greens

Serves 4 as a side dish

You can make this with your favorite greens such as Swiss chard, kale or even spinach.

1   tablespoon olive oil (optional)
1   large bunch greens such as kale or Swiss chard, washed well, not dried
1-2 cloves garlic, finely minced
1   teaspoon chicken flavored broth powder in 3 tablespoons water

Put oil in a large skillet over a medium flame. Add garlic and greens directly to pan, if omitting oil. Greens may barely fit in the pan. Don't worry, as it will shrink down. Cook greens, stirring well until all leaves are slightly wilted and the garlic is no longer raw. Add the broth and water mixture as the greens are cooking. When the liquid is evaporated and the greens are bright green, it's done. Serve hot.

"Unstuffy" Stuffing with Mushrooms and Walnuts

Makes about 12 cups or 6-8 servings

*T*his recipe is best with sourdough bread but whole grain bread works well, too. If you can get Alvarado Street Bakery sprouted sourdough in an uncut loaf it is perfect. If you have fresh chestnuts available, add 1/4 cup chopped instead of the walnuts. This recipe is well suited to dry sautéing the initial ingredients.

1	tablespoon oil
1	cup chopped fresh mushrooms
2	large onions, diced
2	large carrots, shredded
2	stalks celery, finely chopped
2	cloves garlic, minced
4	cups oat bran or other flake cereal
8	cups stale sourdough bread, cubed
1/4	cup minced fresh Italian parsley
1/2	teaspoon fresh rosemary, chopped, or
	1 teaspoon dried rosemary
2	teaspoons fresh sage or 1 tablespoon dried sage
1	teaspoon fresh thyme or 1 tablespoon dried thyme
2	tablespoons chopped walnuts

Freshly ground pepper, to taste
1 1/4 cups vegetable broth

Preheat oven to 350˚ F.

Pour the oil into a large skillet. Add the onions, celery and carrots and cook for 2 minutes. Add the mushrooms and cook 10 more minutes. Add the garlic and cook an additional 5 minutes. Put the vegetable mixture into a bowl and mix in the bread cubes, cereal flakes herbs, nuts, and pepper. Add the broth and mix well.

Coat a baking dish with oil or cooking spray. Cover the dish and bake for 25 to 35 minutes until the stuffing is hot. You can make this in advance and reheat it, or leave it at room temperature for less than 2 hours.

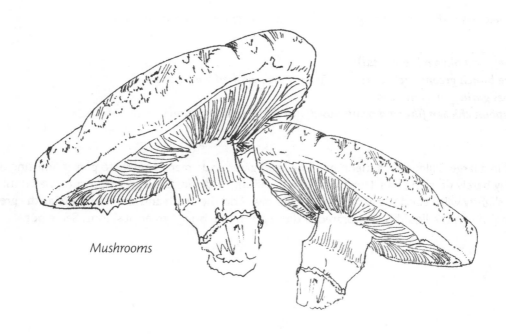

Mushrooms

Fruited Wild Rice

Serves 8 to 10
(Based on a recipe found in Gourmet Vegetarian Feasts, Martha Rose Shulman, Thorsons, 1987)

*S*erve as a side dish or stuff a squash such as kabocha, buttercup or white pumpkin with this mixture. In any case it is delicious.

1 1/2 **cups wild rice**
4 1/2 **cups water**
1 **cup chopped dried raisins, cranberries and tart cherries, or your favorites**
Sherry to cover the dried fruit
2 **small apples, peeled, cored, cut in half crosswise and sliced thinly**
1 **large pear, peeled, cored and sliced**
1/2 **cup slivered almonds**
2 **tablespoons apple juice**
1 **tablespoon honey or maple syrup**
1 **teaspoon cinnamon**
1/2 **teaspoon freshly ground nutmeg**
1/2 **teaspoon allspice**
1/2 **teaspoon cardamom**
1/2 **teaspoon freshly ground black pepper**
Salt and pepper to taste

Cook wild rice in the water for 55 to 60 minutes until the rice grains are split open (or cook in the pressure cooker with 3 cups water for 25 minutes at high pressure with a natural pressure release). When done, drain rice from cooking water and put in a large bowl.

While the rice is cooking, soak the dried fruit in sherry to cover. Drain fruit after 30 minutes and set aside. (You can save the sherry in the refrigerator for future soaking, use it in salad dressing, for a stir-fry or an after dinner drink.)

Heat a large heavy skillet over medium heat and sauté apples, pears and almonds about 2 minutes. Add the apple juice and continue to cook for a few more minutes. Add 1 tablespoon honey, spices, cooked wild rice, drained fruit and salt to taste. Cook together another few minutes, stirring. Correct seasonings, adding lots of pepper if you like it. Remove from heat. Serve mounded on a plate or stuff into a partially pre-baked squash and bake in the oven at 350° F. for 30 to 45 minutes until the squash is thoroughly cooked and the filling is hot.

Potato and Kohlrabi Gratin

Serves 8

I really like kohlrabi, a cruciferous vegetable with a great crunch raw and a mild turnip-like taste when cooked. It makes this plain potato dish more interesting. If kohlrabi is unavailable, you can substitute turnips or rutabaga.

1 1/2 **pounds kohlrabi, tough outer peel removed**
2 1/2 **pounds unpeeled baking potatoes**
2   **tablespoons soy margarine**
1/2   **cup soy Parmesan cheese**
1/2   **cup shredded soy cheese, garlic herb, cheddar or jack-style**
1/2   **teaspoon salt**
1   **teaspoon freshly ground black pepper**
1   **tablespoon fresh minced thyme or dill**
1 1/2 **cups multigrain or soy milk**
1/3   **cup dried, fine breadcrumbs**

Steam kohlrabi over boiling water for 20 to 30 minutes, until tender when pierced with a fork. Do the same with the potatoes. You can do them both at the same time in separate pots with steamer baskets or one and then the other.

When the potatoes are cool, peel them. Slice each vegetable into 1/4-inch thick slices, keeping them separated.

Preheat oven to 350° F.

Choose a gratin dish deep enough to hold 3 layers of sliced vegetables. Spray the dish with oil. Arrange half the potatoes in the bottom of the dish. Sprinkle with 1/3 the soy Parmesan and shredded soy cheese, salt, pepper and thyme. Dot with 1/2 tablespoon butter. Arrange all the kohlrabi on top of the potatoes. Sprinkle with half the remaining cheeses, salt and pepper and thyme. Dot with 1/2 tablespoon margarine. Layer the remaining potato slices on top and sprinkle with the remaining cheese, salt, pepper and thyme. Pour the milk over the vegetables. Put the breadcrumbs on the surface and dot with the remaining 1 tablespoon of margarine.

Place in the oven and bake until the sauce is bubbling and the topping is golden brown, 30 to 40 minutes. Remove from the oven and serve hot or warm, scooping out portions with a spoon.

Guess What This Is?

The name is exotic and the vegetable looks as if it came from another planet. Both of these are good reasons why so many people pass by it and don't give it a second glance. Instead they head for the broccoli, cauliflower and cabbage (which are fellow members of the cruciferous vegetable family).

It's easy to stump a large audience by holding up a kohlrabi and asking if anyone knows what it is. There may only be two in a group of 50 or more that can correctly identify it. Sometimes no one knows which doesn't mean that they haven't seen it.

The round bulb has a root that grows underground but the edible part grows above ground. It can either be light green or purple and has leaves growing up from the bulbous part. It looks otherworldly.

I have been told that one can eat the leaves but I have never found them tender enough to do so. They become part of my compost. You can try cooking them if you like since they will not hurt you. The bulb is the tasty part. And that's only after you peel off the tough outer layer. The firm and crunchy inner flesh has a slight cabbage or turnip flavor, common to most cruciferous vegetables. I mostly eat my kohlrabi raw, but it can be steamed and eaten plain, mashed or mixed with other cooked root vegetables.

My friend Laurie, a confirmed vegetarian, recently saw kohlrabi at a farm stand, but decided not to buy it, since she'd never tried it. Amazingly, at our writer's group, fellow member, Christine, our host and a chef, had kohlrabi recently harvested from her garden in the refrigerator. Laurie got a kohlrabi show-and-tell and a tasting. She liked it and is now a kohlrabi convert. Be adventurous. Don't be afraid to try new and different vegetables.

Kohlrabi

Fall

Red Peppers Stuffed with Quinoa, Squash and Sunflower Seeds

Serves 4

*W*hen preparing this for others, I have been told that it is the first time that some people have eaten cooked bell peppers. The presentation is terrific and they taste great. You can add any other ingredients that you like to the filling. I have used tempeh in it before with great results.

2/3	cup quinoa
1 1/4	cups water
1	tablespoon chicken flavored broth powder
2	tablespoons tamari or Bragg's liquid amino acids
2	tablespoons water
2	large garlic cloves, finely minced, separated
4	large ripe red bell peppers of similar size with large hollows that will stand up easily
1	tablespoon oil
1	medium onion, diced
1	medium sweet red or mildly hot pepper, such as an Anaheim
1	small zucchini or yellow squash, diced
1	large or 2 medium tomatoes, chopped
3	tablespoons chopped fresh parsley and 3 tablespoons other fresh herbs such as basil, oregano, rosemary or thyme
3	tablespoons toasted sunflower seeds
1/2	cup tomato juice
Salt and freshly ground black pepper, to taste	
4	teaspoons grated soy cheese or soy Parmesan cheese

Preheat oven to 375° F. Rinse quinoa well under water in a fine mesh strainer.

Toast quinoa for 1 to 2 minutes in a medium saucepan with a tight fitting lid over medium heat, uncovered. Add the water and broth powder. Raise heat to high and bring the mixture to a boil. Stir and reduce the heat to a simmer. Cover pan and cook for 12 minutes. Remove from heat and let stand for 5 more minutes. If not using immediately, remove quinoa from pan and put into a bowl.

While the grains are cooking, cut the tops off the peppers, and remove the ribs and seeds.

Put the peppers in a steamer basket over simmering water 5 to 10 minutes in a covered pot to soften them a little. (They will not be baking long so need to be precooked.) Remove the steamer basket from the pot and put in a sink. Turn peppers upside down to drain. Set aside.

Add the oil to a sauté pan. Sauté the onion and sweet or mildly hot pepper for about 5 minutes until the onion becomes transparent. Add the diced squash and garlic and sauté over medium heat another 5 minutes until the squash begins to cook. Add tomato and cook another 5 minutes until tomato softens. Remove from heat and add parsley and other herbs to the vegetables. Combine with the cooked grains. Stir in the sunflower seeds. Add salt and pepper to taste. Stuff mixture into the peppers. Place in a baking dish. Pour tomato juice over and around the vegetables.

Bake covered for 10 minutes. Remove cover, sprinkle each pepper with 1 teaspoon cheese and bake another 5 minutes, until filling is hot and peppers are cooked through but not mushy. Serve immediately.

The Vegetable We Love to Say We Hate

Shortly before moving to Sonoma County, I was invited as part of a select group of dietitians, just one from each state, to attend a conference in Minnesota. It was designed to help us learn how to disseminate nutrition information to our local community. I decided that I wanted to promote vegetables. (You can see that I have been at this for a long time.)

I developed a brochure about Brussels sprouts as a mock-up of my idea. I now realize that I was out of my mind to try promoting a vegetable that most people think that they hate. The reality is far different. In fact, the last time that I prepared Brussels sprouts at one of my cooking classes they were gobbled up quickly.

When I was pitching the idea of eating Brussels sprouts, some members of The Sonoma County Farmlands Group affectionately referred to me as the "Brussels sprout woman." That was fine with me. Since then I have come to realize that dislike for this vegetable arises out of improper preparation and cooking procedures.

Undercooked sprouts do not taste good. But when cooked to perfection, and there are a number of ways to do this, they are delectable. No matter how you cook the sprouts, start by cutting off any old outer leaves and the bottom of the stem. Make an X in the stem end. Since this is a cruciferous vegetable, which means it grows like a cross, X marks the spot. Steam the sprouts in the microwave or a pot for just a couple of minutes, or more depending on the rest of the cooking treatment.

One of my favorite ways to cook Brussels sprouts is by cutting them in half and sautéing them in either a dry pan or with a touch of oil, with something sweet like orange juice or maple syrup, and tossing in some chopped nuts.

Or you can halve them, mix with a little olive oil and put them on a baking sheet. Bake at 400° F. for about 20 minutes until cooked through. Season any way you like.

If I am going to cut away the stem and use only the leaves, then I do not precook but add liquid in the cooking process to help assure that they are cooked thoroughly.

Brussels sprouts are wonderful paired with nuts, such as almonds, chestnuts and hazelnuts (also known as filberts), which arrive on the scene around the same time in late fall into the winter. Be creative and make up your own recipe for one of America's most hated vegetables. You just might have to cross it off your "do not like" list.

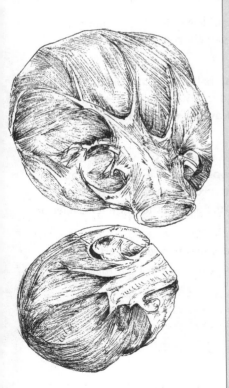

Brussels Sprouts

Stuffed Swiss Chard

Makes 6 main-dish servings of 2 rolls each

*T*his is a cross between dolmas, stuffed grape leaves, and stuffed cabbage rolls. No matter what, it's tasty. Be sure to choose leaves with narrow stems, as it will make stuffing easier.

2	Tbs. olive oil, divided
1	cup brown rice or brown and wild rice blend, rinsed well
1	cinnamon stick
2	cups water
1	large bunch Swiss chard with at least 18 leaves, 12 of which must be intact, washed well but not dried
1/2	cup chopped onion
3	Tbs. toasted pine nuts
1/4	cup golden raisins or currants
2	Tbs. lemon juice

Salt and freshly ground black pepper to taste

2	cups tomato sauce
2	Tbs. golden raisins or currants

With heat off, pour 1 tablespoon oil in medium-sized saucepan. Add rice; stir to coat with oil. Add cinnamon stick and water; bring to boil. Cover; reduce heat to simmer and cook 40 minutes. Remove from heat; let stand 5 minutes before uncovering. Remove cinnamon stick.

While the rice is cooking, steam or blanch 12 intact Swiss chard leaves for 2 to 3 minutes so they will be more pliable. Remove thick stems from steamed leaves; chop stems. Set steamed leaves and chopped stems aside.

Remove and discard stems from uncooked chard leaves. Chop half of the uncooked chard leaves. Heat remaining tablespoon of oil in skillet. Add onion and steamed, chopped stems; sauté over medium heat for 1 to 2 minutes. Add chopped uncooked leaves, pine nuts and raisins or currants. Cook until chard is wilted, about 3 to 4 minutes.

Combine rice mixture with chard mixture. Add lemon juice; stir well. Season with salt and pepper. Line a thick-bottomed skillet or pot with remaining uncooked chard leaves. Now gather the 12 intact, blanched leaves. Take one leaf and put 1/3 cup rice mixture on bottom third of leaf, stem side toward you. Fold sides of leaf in then roll tightly upward. Put into the leaf-lined skillet or pot. Repeat with remaining steamed leaves.

Mix tomato sauce with 2 tablespoons raisins or currants; pour mixture over stuffed leaves. Cover skillet or pot; cook on low heat 30 minutes. Let the stuffed leaves sit for a few minutes before serving with a bit of sauce over each roll-up.

Swiss Chard

Chard of a Different Color

When my son Shane was in fifth grade his teacher Nathan asked me for a recipe to cook the chard that was grown in their school garden. I suggested that he prepare it the way that I do for Simple Greens (see page 55).

Shortly thereafter Shane came home from school and said, "I really like chard, do you think that you could buy it for me?"

This was a memorable moment - my son asking me to cook him vegetables. And, I of course, resoundingly said, "Yes. I'll get some this weekend at the farmer's market."

I inquired about Shane's sudden interest in chard. He explained that Nathan had cooked chard from the school garden in class that day.

I got a detailed description about how Nathan prepared the chard with olive oil, garlic and a little lemon juice so I could repeat the process. It was very similar to my recipe but with the addition of lemon juice.

I would have made Shane chard immediately but I didn't have any since I can't eat it. The oxalates it contains makes my mouth feel as if I had eaten an unripe persimmon (if you have ever done this you know how awful that can be). Many people like it and Shane is one of them.

On my next trip to the farmer's market, I bought some beautiful young chard leaves in all colors of the rainbow. After all, Santa Rosa was the home of the famous horticulturist Luther Burbank who developed rainbow chard.

At home I was excited to be preparing a vegetable that Shane had requested. Shane came into the kitchen and directed me through the cooking process, telling me when to add the oil and garlic, how long to cook the chard and "don't forget to squeeze on the lemon juice". I was sure that he'd just love the chard that I made.

Wrong. He told me that Nathan knows how to cook it better (I expected that). Then he added, "I only like the red chard."

On my next attempt I bought only red chard but that didn't measure up to Nathan's, either. Shane still eats Swiss chard once in a while when I remember to buy it. But only the red-leaf kind.

Squash Custard

Serves 6

I like being able to use a vegetable in dessert. After all, isn't that what pumpkin pie is all about?

Vegetable cooking spray
1	tablespoon maple syrup
1	tablespoon Sucanat or brown sugar
1	medium winter squash, such as Delicata or Carnivale, baked until soft to equal 1 1/2 cups mashed squash
1	box Mori Nu silken lite firm tofu
3-5	tablespoons maple syrup
1	teaspoon vanilla extract
1/2	teaspoon freshly grated nutmeg
1	teaspoon ground cinnamon
3	tablespoons frozen apple juice concentrate
1/4	cup vanilla rice, oat, almond or other nondairy milk
1	teaspoon agar agar powder

Preheat oven to 350° F.

Coat six ramekins or glass custard cups with vegetable cooking spray. Mix maple syrup with Sucanat. Spoon 1 teaspoon of mixture into each ramekin. Put 1/2-inch of water into a large baking pan and set the ramekins into the pan.

Put the mashed squash, maple syrup, cinnamon, nutmeg and tofu into a food processor. Blend until smooth.

In a small saucepan, combine the apple juice concentrate, rice milk and agar agar over medium to high heat. Bring to a simmer, stirring often, and simmer for 2-3 minutes. Pour the agar mixture into the tofu mixture and process well.

Spoon 1/6th of the mixture into each ramekin, smoothing the top with a spoon.

Bake 40 to 50 minutes until custard is set. Let cool slightly before serving.

If you like, garnish with raspberries or kiwi slices.

Spiced Sweet Potato Pie

Serves 8

*W*ho says that dessert can't be delicious and good for you too? This pie really disproves that theory. Make it whenever you feel like indulging and eating well, too. I let my son eat it for breakfast if there is any left over.

1	package ginger cookies or enough to equal 1 1/2 cups crumbs
1	tablespoon canola oil
1	tablespoon maple syrup
2	pounds garnet yams, baked until soft, cooled and peeled
3/4	cup vanilla almond, rice or soy drink
1	tablespoon egg replacer or 4 ounces silken tofu
4	medjool dates plus 4 more for garnish
1	teaspoon cinnamon
1/2	teaspoon powdered ginger
1/4	teaspoon freshly grated nutmeg
1/4	teaspoon allspice

Preheat oven to 350° F.

Process cookies in the food processor until they are crumbled. Add the oil and maple syrup and process again until the mixture seems sticky.

Press the crumbs into a pie plate with damp fingers. Chill for 10 minutes and then prebake in the oven for 4 minutes. Let cool for at least 10 minutes before filling.

Put the peeled yams into the food processor. Add the remaining ingredients, except the 4 dates for garnish, and process until the mixture is completely smooth and the dates in it are finely chopped. Pour this into the cooled pie shell.

Bake for 1 hour. Slice the 4 dates in half lengthwise and position them on top of the baked pie. Let the pie cool slightly before serving. Cut into 8 pieces.

"The act of putting into your mouth what the earth has grown is perhaps your most direct interaction with the earth."

Frances Moore Lappe, author,
'Diet for a Small Planet'

Winter

*T*he selection of available vegetables narrows but doesn't disappear. One learns to become creative with broccoli, spinach, cabbage and greens. In the past few years the variety of cauliflower has grown with traditional white joined by green, orange and purple. The taste and texture of each varies and their hues add a bright accent to the general green and white color scheme of winter vegetables. And these cauliflower unlike their colorful relatives such as purple beans and broccoli, retain its color when cooked.

If you can find a braising mix, a combination of baby winter greens, try it. Eating winter vegetables helps boost your winter health. You can't go wrong by eating lots of green, leafy vegetables. They taste best after the first frost when their sweetness becomes evident.

Other winter sweeties include sweet potatoes, carrots, beets and parsnips. You can also enjoy Jerusalem artichokes, celery root, daikon radish, kohlrabi, potatoes, winter squash and turnips. They all keep well under proper conditions, which is why there used to be root cellars. These hearty roots and tubers are versatile and incredibly tasty although some are downright ugly. Don't let that deter you. Eat your veggies.

Wild Mushroom Ravioli

Serves 4-6 as an appetizer

I absolutely love mushrooms, but my husband does not, so I use them often in my classes. Rather than make the ravioli dough by hand, I use potsticker or wonton wrappers for the dough.

1-2	tablespoons olive oil
1/2	cup chopped shallots or onions
2	pounds assorted wild mushrooms such as shiitake, chanterelles, oyster or even some crimini (to cut the cost), finely chopped
1-2	teaspoons Bragg's liquid amino acids or tamari
1/2	box Mori Nu or 6 ounces other silken firm tofu
2	teaspoons Organic Gourmet wild mushroom broth paste or mild miso
2	tablespoons chopped Italian parsley or cilantro
1/4	teaspoon freshly ground pepper
1	package potsticker or wonton wrappers

Heat the oil in a sauté pan. Add the shallots or onions and sauté over medium heat for 3 minutes. Add the finely chopped mushrooms and sauté until the mushrooms start to release their juices. Continue to sauté until the mushrooms are fairly dry. Add the Bragg's or tamari. Stir and remove from the heat.

Process the tofu in the food processor with the mushroom paste, parsley and pepper. Stir in the mushrooms.

Take 1 wrapper and place 2 tablespoons of filling on it. You can either fold over the wrapper and seal the edges with water, or if you want larger ravioli you can place another wrapper on top and seal the edges with water. Let sit only for a few minutes before putting into boiling water or they may get dried out. Cook the ravioli for 3 to 4 minutes, until the wrappers are cooked through.

Serve with a sauce on the side or use a mushroom-based salad dressing or marinade.

Mediterranean Greens

Serves 4-6 as an appetizer on toasts or 4 as a side dish

I just love greens, especially in the winter when they taste the best. Here they are paired with tangy, sweet and salty: a splash of balsamic vinegar, raisins or currants, and olives.

1   **tablespoon olive oil**
1/2   **cup finely minced onion**
2   **pounds greens such as kale, chard, mustard, collards, washed but not dried and center ribs removed, cut finely**
1/4   **cup golden raisins or currants**
Water or broth, as needed
1/4   **cup finely chopped kalamata olives**
1-2   **tablespoons balsamic vinegar**
1   **tablespoon extra virgin olive oil**
Freshly ground black pepper, to taste

Heat the oil in a sauté pan over medium heat. Add the onion and sauté for 3-4 minutes, until it turns translucent. Add the greens and sauté for 1 minute. Add the raisins or currants and cook until the greens turn bright green. Stir in the olives. If the greens get dry while cooking, add broth or water 1 tablespoon at a time being careful not to let the mixture get too liquid. Remove from the heat and let cool a bit. Add the balsamic vinegar and olive oil. Taste and adjust seasonings, adding more vinegar, oil or pepper if necessary. Serve on crostini (Italian toasts), see page 90.

Washing Greens

An important step with any greens, salad or cooking, is to be sure that they are thoroughly clean. The best way to do this is to put them in a sink with a stopper and run water over them, filling the sink. Then remove the greens, rinse the dirt and debris out of the sink and repeat the process until your greens are clean. Greens can get especially dirty and sandy in the winter. I have not yet met anyone who likes to eat dirt in his or her food.

If you are making salad, use a salad spinner and dry the greens. If you plan to cook the greens, leave some water clinging to the leaves, as this will help them steam in the pan.

Greens are packed with nutrition. The incredible variety can keep you eating healthy for days. Try them all if you can, to decide which are your favorites. They include mizuna; tatsoi; mild or hot red mustard; collards; red Russian, dinosaur (also known as lacinata), curly, purple, peacock or other varieties of kale; Swiss chard; spinach, beet, turnip and other greens. Time to grab my garlic and pan and cook up a batch of greens.

Jerusalem Artichoke Salad
with Arugula and Cranberry Vinaigrette

Serves 4 to 6

I love the crunch of Jerusalem artichokes, which are also sometimes called sunchokes. They contain a substance called inulin, which is a starch that is digested differently than other starches. Inulin is supposed to be better for diabetics. This salad combines crunchy, sweet, tart, bitter and a bite from the onion. When cranberries are in season, freeze an extra bag and use them as you need them.

1/2	cup water or vegetable broth
1	tablespoon cornstarch
1/3	cup orange juice
3	tablespoons balsamic or cranberry vinegar
1	teaspoon Dijon mustard
1	pressed clove garlic
1/4	cup fresh or thawed frozen cranberries
1	pound of Jerusalem artichokes, also known as sunchokes
4	cups arugula
1	small head soft lettuce, like bibb or Boston
1/4	cup dried cranberries
1/4	red onion, finely sliced

Combine water and cornstarch in a small saucepan. Bring almost to a boil, until thickened, about 5 minutes. Remove from heat and let cool.

In a blender, combine the above mixture with the orange juice, balsamic vinegar, mustard, garlic and the fresh cranberries. Mix well and refrigerate until needed.

Scrub the Jerusalem artichokes well and cut into thin slices. You may peel them if you like. (If you do, get more than a pound as there is quite a bit of waste.)

Wash the arugula well and tear into bite size pieces. Do the same with the lettuce, and then mix together in a large bowl.

Serve by placing sunchoke slices on top of greens. Sprinkle cranberries and onions over salad. Drizzle some dressing on and save the rest to pass.

You may also serve this salad on individual plates, arranging it in the same manner.

Sweetheart of a Salad

Serves 4

This winter combination provides a beautiful and tasty start to almost any meal. The silkiness of the avocado contrasts well with the grapefruit.

8	**cups spinach, washed and dried**
1	**large pink or white grapefruit, peeled and sectioned (save the remains)**
1/2	**avocado, sliced**
2	**tablespoons rice vinegar**
1	**teaspoon sweetener such as Sucanat or sugar**
1	**teaspoon tamari**
2	**tablespoons sesame seeds, toasted**

Place spinach in a bowl or separate and divide among 4 individual plates. Arrange grapefruit slices and avocado over spinach.

To make dressing, squeeze juice out of leftover grapefruit and mix with rice vinegar, sweetener and tamari. Set aside.

Pour sesame seeds into a blender. Grind until seeds are powdered. Add grapefruit juice dressing mixture and combine, blending completely. Pour over salad. Serve immediately.

Avocados - The Vegetable Butter

I tasted my first avocado while I was in 4th grade. I can remember my teacher, Mrs. Stad, asking if anyone had ever tried one. I was one of few who ever had and the experience had been recent. Most kids in New York never saw an avocado, but my mother's aunt in Florida had a tree. So my Mom was familiar with avocados. She saw one at the store and wanted me to try one. I could not understand an avocado's appeal. It was watery and slimy, not qualities that appeal to a child, at least not to me.

It wasn't until I was 21 and traveling on a cross-country car trip with my sister, Donna, that I tasted an avocado worth eating. We were with a fellow traveler in Oregon, who offered us a taste of a perfectly ripe Haas avocado. It was heaven in my mouth. From then on I craved California avocados, but they weren't available in Florida. And as I knew, Florida avocados are a different fruit altogether.

Luckily Donna went to UCLA law school and lived in Los Angeles. Whenever I went to visit, at least a couple of times a year, I tucked a few avocados into my carry-on bag for safe keeping on the trip to Florida. My bag was always being inspected at check-through (this was obviously before tight airport security). I still wonder whether they thought the avocados were grenades. Once, my avocado inspection resulted in such a delay, that my seat in coach was given away. Fortunately, it resulted in my being upgraded to first class. That only increased my fondness for avocados.

Despite how much I enjoy eating them, I still limit myself to one avocado a week because along with their vitamins, minerals and sublime taste, they pack a serious dose of calories and fat (even if it is monounsaturated). I savor every creamy, delicious bite. My favorite ways to eat an avocado is sliced in a salad or on a sandwich or spread on whole grain toast with a sprinkle of gomashio or toasted sesame seeds.

Cabbage and Red Apple Slaw

Serves 6

*T*his takes just a few minutes in your food processor. Since cabbage, apples and carrots are almost always available, you can make this anytime, but it's especially refreshing in the winter, when green salad might not seem as appealing. It's terrific to bring to potlucks, since you'll be sure to have vegetables to eat.

1 1/2	**pounds green cabbage, finely shredded**
1	**red apple, grated**
1	**large carrot, grated**
1 1/2	**tablespoons maple syrup**
2-3	**tablespoons apple cider vinegar**
1	**tablespoon Dijon mustard**
1/2	**teaspoon sea salt**

Quarter the cabbage, remove and discard the central white core. Shred the cabbage by cutting very thin slices along the length of each quarter. You should have about 6 cups. You can use the shredding disk of the food processor for this.

Place the shredded cabbage in a large bowl. Toss in the carrots and apple. In a small jar, combine the maple syrup, vinegar, mustard and salt. Shake vigorously and pour over the cabbage. Taste and add more vinegar if desired.

Refrigerate for at least half an hour before serving.

Spinach Salad with Warm Sesame Dressing

Serves 4

*T*his dressing can also be used without being heated, without the garlic and ginger unless you like them uncooked. The warm dressing slightly wilts the spinach, making it easier to eat when it is cool outside.

6	**cups spinach leaves, washed and drained**
1	**teaspoon canola oil**
1	**clove garlic, minced**
1	**teaspoon minced ginger**
1/4	**cup orange juice**
1	**tablespoon reduced sodium tamari**
1	**tablespoon honey or other sweetener**
2	**teaspoons sesame oil**
2	**tablespoons toasted sesame seeds, for garnish**

Put washed spinach leaves in a bowl or on individual plates.

Heat a sauté pan over medium heat. Add canola oil, garlic and ginger and sauté for 2-3 minutes. Slowly and carefully add the orange juice to avoid sputtering oil. Add the remaining ingredients except sesame seeds and heat until hot. Pour over the spinach. Garnish with the toasted sesame seeds. Serve immediately.

Ma and Pa

No, I didn't grow up where I referred to my parents as Ma and Pa. But maybe Cliff Silva did and that's why his business is called Ma and Pa's Garden. Cliff is a short, elfish looking man; paired with Joy, his tall, blonde wife of many years they make a slightly odd couple. Cliff credits Joy with doing most of the work at the garden. She used to help sell their produce at the farmer's markets, but I haven't seen her much lately. She must be busy at home tending the plants.

Cliff is a funny guy. He won't hesitate to tell you that his produce is the "best". I certainly won't argue the point, even if I could. He takes pride in the cleanliness of his celery roots, how his peppers gleam colorfully in the sun, or the sweetness of his broccoli shoots. Did I forget to mention his boasting about his potatoes, fresh dug this morning?

Cliff has spent the past 30 years as a landscaper in the area. His crops are not substantially different from many other local farmers but there's only one Cliff. He's always cheerful and friendly, telling me about what he has that day that I just have to try.

One Saturday, I stopped by to see the last of the orange cauliflower. I had heard about it for weeks but hadn't managed to get to the market early enough to buy it. The one remaining head was small. I asked for more. "That's all there is, Jill," Cliff told me. "Why don't you just take it?" he offered. So I did. It wound up as an important ingredient in Red Rice Salad with Lemony Roasted Cauliflower.

Red Rice Salad with Lemony Roasted Cauliflower

Serves 4

If you can get colored cauliflower, orange, green, or purple, it makes this dish look even more interesting. But even if you use traditional white cauliflower, it will taste great.

3	**cups cauliflower, steamed for**
	1 1/2 minutes on stovetop or microwave
2	**teaspoons olive oil**
1	**teaspoon lemon olive oil**
Salt and pepper to taste	
1 1/2	**cups water**
1/2	**teaspoon salt**
1	**cup Bhutanese red rice**
	(if using other check package directions)
1-2	**tablespoons lemon juice**
1	**tablespoon olive oil (optional)**
Salt and pepper to taste	

Preheat the oven to 400 degrees F.

Put the cauliflower in a glass baking dish and toss with the olive oil, salt and pepper. Cover the dish and bake for 20 to 25 minutes until the cauliflower is cooked through but still firm. Let cauliflower cool.

Bring the water and salt to a boil and stir in the rice. Reduce the heat to a simmer. Cover tightly and cook for 20 minutes. Remove from heat and let sit for 5 minutes. Put in a bowl and let cool.

Combine the cooked rice with the cauliflower. Add lemon juice, olive oil, if using and salt and pepper to taste. Chill, if desired or serve at room temperature.

Spicy Greens Salad with Baked Tofu and Roasted Shiitake Mushrooms

Serves 4-6

*R*oasting really brings out the flavor in the vegetables and tofu. This salad makes a great lunch salad or a heartier-than-usual dinner salad that goes well with light soup. In addition to great taste, this salad has immune system boosting properties. You can use crimini mushrooms as a substitute for shiitake to save money but they don't taste as good or boost your immune system.

1/2	**pound shiitake mushrooms, stems removed, cut into slices**
1	**large onion, cut in half lengthwise and cut into slices**
1/2	**pound firm tofu, drained and cut into small cubes**
1	**tablespoon canola oil**
1	**teaspoon toasted sesame oil**
3	**tablespoons tamari or soy sauce**
2	**teaspoons Sucanat or brown sugar**
1	**clove garlic, minced**
1	**teaspoon grated ginger**

Dressing

3	**tablespoons rice vinegar**
1-2	**tablespoons plum or other sweet Asian sauce**
1	**tablespoon tamari**
1	**teaspoon toasted sesame oil**
	Pinch of crushed red pepper or a small spoonful of chili paste
6-8	**cups baby Asian mix or other dark and spicy greens - usually includes mizuna, arugula, baby mustard**
3	**tablespoons toasted sesame seeds**

Preheat the oven to 350° F.

Combine the canola and sesame oils, tamari, Sucanat, garlic and ginger in a small bowl.

Put the mushrooms, onion and tofu in a large baking dish. Be sure not to crowd the ingredients. Use 2 dishes if you need to. Pour the mixture in the bowl over the mushrooms, onions and tofu and let marinate for at least 15 minutes. Then bake in the oven for 15 minutes. Turn the tofu cubes and check mushrooms. Continue baking another 10 to 15 minutes. Be sure that mushrooms are thoroughly cooked. Remove mushrooms, onions and tofu from the oven and let cool a bit.

Whisk together the dressing ingredients: rice vinegar, plum sauce, tamari, sesame oil and crushed red pepper or chili paste in a small bowl. Taste and add more tamari or vinegar, if needed.

Toss the greens with the dressing and arrange them in a bowl or on individual plates. Arrange the mushrooms, onion and tofu on the greens. Garnish with the sesame seeds.

Curried Pear and Squash Soup

Serves 4-6

Squash tastes great paired with pear. If you like, you can add a pinch of cayenne for contrast, in addition to the lemon juice in the recipe. You can always use broth instead of the water and broth powder mixture. This soup has become a holiday and winter staple for me.

3	delicata squash, roasted until soft in the oven to equal 1 1/2-2 cups
1	small onion, diced
1	medium D'anjou or comice pear, peeled and cut into chunks
2-3	teaspoons or more curry powder
2	tablespoons vegetarian chicken flavored broth powder
4	cups water
1	tablespoon lemon juice
1/2	teaspoon salt
	Freshly ground black pepper
2	tablespoons fresh parsley or cilantro, chopped

Cut the squash in half and place cut side down in a glass baking dish with 1/2 inch water. You may need more than one dish. Roast the squash until a knife is easily inserted into the squash, about 25 minutes. Cool and scrape pulp from skin.

Heat the stockpot over medium heat. Dry sauté the onion for 5 minutes until it softens. Add the pear and curry powder and sauté for 2 minutes. Stir in the broth powder and water and simmer for 10 minutes until the pear is soft. Add the roasted squash and simmer for another 10 minutes to blend flavors. Using a hand blender, puree until desired consistency. Taste and add the lemon juice, salt and pepper. Garnish with parsley or cilantro. Serve hot.

Soup's On

In the fifteen plus years that I have lived in Sonoma County a number of farmers have come and gone at the Santa Rosa Farmer's Market. The most recent departure is Larry Rogers who headed to Washington State.

A large red-haired guy, Larry was always cheerful and generous. When his apples, peppers and squash were in season he would show up at the market no matter what the weather. He sold other produce too, all grown organically. That was important to him and also to me.

Larry and I would often laugh about the number of people that would ask him if his winter squash were edible. He thought that more people bought them as decorations than as food. I must admit that they are beautiful and add color to a winter table, but the taste is what keeps me coming back.

And just so you know, they do not all taste the same. If you've only tried butternut or acorn squash it is time to branch out. My favorite squash is delicata but I also like buttercup, red kuri, sunshine and blue Hubbard, among others.

Here are some ideas for what to do with your squash. Invite friends over for a big pot of soup. Steam a few different squash varieties in one pot and do a side by side taste test. Or peel and cut them in cubes and roast them. Taste them all side by side to compare their particular appeal. Imagine chunks of creamy sweetness in chili, soup, stew or even dessert; play and experiment.

Sometimes the best squash is that which has been given to you. Stewart, a fellow mushroom hunter, grows huge banana squash. Every time I have seen him since the squash-harvesting season, which is usually in late September or early October, he has been giving away squash. While this is not my favorite kind of squash, because it is not especially sweet or dense, banana squash works well to fill up the soup pot, letting the flavor of the delicatas that I prefer shine through. Never overlook the gift of squash, for soup you shall have.

Lemony Lentil and Potato Chowder

Serves 6-8

I love lentils and the red ones break down so nicely but unfortunately turn yellow when cooked. This is comfort food at its best. The lemon and mint also makes it incredibly refreshing and fresh tasting, something not always easy to do mid-winter.

1	tablespoon olive oil
1	medium onion, sliced
1	tablespoon minced garlic
1/4	teaspoon cayenne pepper
2	cups red lentils
6	cups water mixed with 3 teaspoons soup and stock mix or 6 cups vegetable broth
3	cups unpeeled diced potatoes (red look nice but any will work)
1	cup chopped greens like kale, mustard, chard, collards or sorrel
1	teaspoon lemon zest
4	tablespoons lemon juice
1/4	cup chopped mint

Salt and freshly ground black pepper, to taste

Heat the oil over medium heat in a large stockpot. Add onion and sauté for 3 to 4 minutes until it begins to soften. Stir in the garlic and cayenne and cook for 1 minute more. Add the lentils, broth and potatoes. Bring the mixture to a boil, then reduce to a simmer. Simmer, covered, for about 25 minutes or until the lentils and potatoes are tender.

Puree the mixture with a hand blender. Add the greens and cook 5 more minutes until they are wilted. Stir in the lemon zest and juice and the mint. Add salt and pepper, to taste. Serve hot.

Maple Vinegar Sautéed Parsnips

Serves 4

Parsnips are white and look like carrots but they don't really taste like carrots since they are much sweeter. Here they get a sweet and sour treatment with the addition of balsamic vinegar and maple syrup. Be sure that the parsnips get cooked through but not mushy. If you've only tried parsnips in soup, this is your opportunity to put them on your plate.

1	tablespoon oil
2	pounds parsnips, all about the same size, cut into thin slices
2	tablespoons water or broth
4	tablespoons balsamic vinegar
2	tablespoons maple syrup
1/2	teaspoon salt or less, to taste

Freshly ground pepper

Steam the parsnip slices over simmering water for about 5 minutes.

Heat oil in a medium size skillet. Add the parsnips. Sauté for about 3 minutes. When parsnips begin to stick add the water. Sauté for about 5 more minutes. When parsnips start softening and are almost cooked, add the salt, vinegar and maple syrup. Cook over medium heat, stirring occasionally, until the mixture forms a sauce. Serve hot with a sprinkling of freshly ground pepper.

Pasta with Greens, Herbs and Olives

Serves 4-6

I attribute greens with maintaining my health throughout the winter. Combine them with herbs and olives and it is a sure winner. Here, the lemon juice, garlic and herbs add some punch. If you follow the McDougall diet, dry sauté, then add 3 tablespoons broth as needed.

8	cups finely chopped greens such as kale, chard, beet or arugula
1/2	teaspoon salt
1	pound fresh fettucine or linguine, plain or flavored
3	tablespoons extra virgin olive oil
6	cloves garlic, minced
14	Nicoise, Gaeta or Kalamata olives, pitted and coarsely chopped
1-2	tablespoons fresh lemon juice
1	teaspoon lemon zest

Pinch of crushed red pepper flakes
Salt and pepper, to taste

3	tablespoons chopped fresh herbs: marjoram (or oregano), thyme and parsley

Grated soy Parmesan, to taste

Set a large pot on the stove to boil. When it boils, add the greens and salt and boil for 2 minutes. Add the fettucine and cook according to directions (usually for 2-4 minutes) until it is al dente. Before draining, add 1/4 cup pasta cooking water to the sauté pan that has the sauce.

While the water is coming to a boil, heat 2 tablespoons of the olive oil in a sauté pan over medium heat. Add the garlic and sauté for about 2 minutes, being careful not to let it brown. Lower the heat and add the olives and lemon juice. You will then be adding some cooking water, as directed above. Add the drained pasta and greens to the sauté pan with the remaining tablespoon of olive oil, salt, pepper, crushed pepper, lemon zest and the fresh herbs. Heat through. Serve hot, sprinkled with cheese.

Beet, Potato and Leek Gratin

Serves 8

*T*he bright pink color of this dish is remarkable. Once you have done the initial preparation you can pop this into the oven and move on to other kitchen activities such as making a great salad to go with dinner.

McDougallers will leave out the oil at all steps. To sauté leeks, start with a dry pan but add a tablespoon of liquid after 2-3 minutes. Don't oil the pan or drizzle oil on top of the crumbs. You may want to cover, bake for 25 minutes, remove the cover and sprinkle breadcrumbs on top for final cooking. The crumbs will not get especially brown.

3	pounds beets, unpeeled, cut in halves or quarters, if large
1 1/2	pounds Yellow Finn or Yukon Gold potatoes, unpeeled
3	large leeks, cut lengthwise, cleaned well and cut into 3-inch pieces
3	tablespoons oil
1/2	cup grated soy Parmesan cheese (regular or soy)
1/4	cup grated nondairy or Gruyere cheese
1	teaspoon salt
1	teaspoon freshly ground black pepper
1	tablespoon minced fresh rosemary
1 1/2	cups nondairy milk, like oat, multigrain, rice or soy milk
1/2	cup fine dried bread crumbs, preferably homemade with whole grain bread

Preheat the oven to 375° F.

Place beets on a steamer rack and steam over boiling water until tender when pierced with a fork, about 20-30 minutes. Steam the potatoes in the same way. When the vegetables are cool enough to handle, peel them and cut them into 1/4-inch slices, keeping them separated by type. (Do not mix the beets and potatoes.)

While the beets and potatoes are steaming, add 1 tablespoon oil to a sauté pan. (McDougallers, start with a dry pan, then add 1 tablespoon liquid after just a few minutes.) Cook leeks over medium heat until they start to wilt.

Combine the 2 cheeses, salt, pepper and rosemary in a bowl.

Oil a 2 1/2 quart shallow baking dish or gratin dish.

Arrange half the beets in the bottom of the dish. Sprinkle with 1/3 of the cheese mixture. Arrange all of the potatoes over the beets. Sprinkle with another 1/3 of the cheese. Arrange the leeks over the potatoes. Layer the remaining beets over the leeks and sprinkle with the remaining cheese. Pour the milk over the top of the vegetables. Put the breadcrumbs over the top and drizzle with the remaining 1 tablespoon oil.

Place the dish in the oven. Bake until the sauce is bubbling and the topping is golden brown, about 30 to 40 minutes. Remove from the oven and serve hot or warm, scooping out the mixture with a spoon.

Note: This looks especially nice if you can find a variety of beets such as golden, chiogga (red or pink and white striped inside) or white.

Spinach, Leek and Mushroom Quiche with an Oat Crust

Serves 4-6

*N*o one will guess that the crust is made from oats. It's easy to vary the ingredients but you have to be careful not to add anything too wet. You can also make this without a crust - a tip for McDougallers. Or use your favorite fat-free crust recipe that requires baking.

1	cup rolled oats
1/3	cup oat bran
3	tablespoons Spectrum Spread, soy margarine or oil
4-5	tablespoons cold water
	Vegetable cooking spray
1	cup chopped leeks
1/4	pound mushrooms, cut into slices, save 8 slices for garnish
1	10 ounce package frozen chopped spinach, thawed
1	box Mori Nu lite firm or extra firm silken tofu
2/3	cup soy or other nondairy milk
1/2	cup soy mozzarella, shredded
1/4	cup soy Parmesan
1/2	teaspoon each dried dill and thyme
1/2	teaspoon salt
1/2	teaspoon freshly ground black pepper

Preheat oven to 375° F.

Spray a 9-inch pie pan with cooking spray.

Combine oats and oat bran. Cut in the spread or margarine until the mixture is the size of coarse cornmeal. Add water one tablespoon at a time and combine mixture with a fork. Continue until it forms a ball. It will be sticky. Put the ball of dough on a piece of wax paper. Top with another piece of wax paper and roll out with a rolling pin until it is the size of your pie pan. Remove one piece of wax paper. Place crust on pie pan. Press dough into pan with wax paper, then remove paper. Bake for 7 minutes. Then let cool.

Meanwhile, spray a nonstick pan with cooking spray. Add the leeks and sauté for a minute or two. Add the mushrooms and sauté for another 5 minutes until the mushrooms release their liquid and turn brown. Remove from heat and let cool. Then put into the bottom of the oat crust.

Squeeze the water out of the thawed spinach by putting it in a towel or cheesecloth and squeezing. Put the spinach, tofu, cheeses, herbs, salt and pepper into a blender and blend for about 30 seconds until the mixture is smooth. Pour on top of the vegetables in the quiche crust. Arrange mushroom slices on top of the filling in a clock pattern.

Bake for 30 to 35 minutes or until a knife inserted near the center of the quiche comes out clean. Remove from oven and let sit for 5 minutes. Serve hot.

Shepherd's Pie

Serves 4-6

*W*hile I am sure that this is a far cry from the traditional version served in England, it is a great vegetarian substitute. The recipe is quite flexible. You can add celery, corn, or other vegetables to this dish. The basic requirements are a stew-like underpart and mashed potatoes on top.

1	tablespoon oil
1	medium onion, diced
2	medium carrots, diced
1	package vegetarian ground beef substitute such as Yves or Lightlife
1	cup canned diced tomatoes
1	teaspoon dried thyme
1/4	teaspoon rosemary
1	tablespoon tamari
1/2	teaspoon ground black pepper
1	cup frozen green peas
1/2	cup frozen corn (optional)
3	large potatoes, peeled and cut into chunks
2/3	cup water
1	tablespoon chicken flavored broth powder

Salt to taste
Water or soy milk, as needed

Preheat the oven to 350° F.

Add the oil to a medium sauté pan over medium heat. Sauté the onion for 2 minutes, then add the carrots and sauté another 3 minutes. Add the veggie "ground" beef, the tomatoes, herbs, tamari and pepper. Cook for about 5 minutes. Remove from the heat and stir in the peas.

While you are cooking the above mixture, cook the potatoes to make mashed potatoes. I pressure cook them in the water for 4 minutes (see recipe on Page 116), then add salt and liquid, as needed.

Lightly oil a 1 to 2-quart casserole dish. Put the veggie mixture on the bottom and spoon the potatoes on top. Bake in the oven for 20 minutes. To brown the potatoes, place under the broiler for 3 minutes. Serve hot.

Layered Polenta Casserole

Serves 6-8

*A*lthough there are 2 parts to this recipe, you can make this quite easily with already prepared, or precooked, polenta and store bought tomato sauce with vegetables. Whether you cook from scratch or use pre-made, this is a terrific dish. What you choose to do will depend upon how much time you have although the polenta is much better when you make it yourself.

4	cups water
1	teaspoon salt
1 1/4	cups coarsely ground cornmeal
1/3	cup sundried tomato pieces or bits
	(cut whole ones with scissors, if you need to)

Pinch of cayenne (optional)

3	tablespoons minced fresh Italian parsley
1	tablespoon olive oil
1	medium onion, diced
3	cloves garlic, minced
1	cup mushroom, chopped fine
8	chopped kalamata olives
1	28 ounce can crushed tomatoes
1	tablespoon Italian seasoning
1	tablespoon balsamic vinegar
2	tablespoons chopped Italian parsley
1 1/2	cups grated soy or other cheese
1/4	cup soy Parmesan

Bring the water to a boil in a saucepan. Add the salt. Stir in the cornmeal and the tomato bits. Reduce the heat to a simmer and stir frequently to prevent sticking. Cook until the polenta is thick. Add the cayenne and parsley. Remove from the heat and pour into a sheet pan, spreading it thin. Refrigerate for at least 30 minutes, until cooled and firm. Then cut into rectangles that will fit into your casserole dish.

While the polenta is cooling, add the olive oil to a sauté pan over medium heat. Add the onion and sauté for 5 minutes. Add the garlic and mushrooms and sauté for another 5 minutes, until the mushrooms are cooked through. Add the tomatoes and Italian seasoning. Cook for about 10 minutes, until the flavors have blended. Remove from the heat and add the balsamic vinegar and parsley.

Preheat the oven to 400° F.

Lightly spray a casserole with oil.

Put 1 cup of sauce on the bottom of the casserole. Layer the polenta rectangles into the casserole. Combine the mozzarella and Parmesan. Sprinkle one third of the cheese over the polenta. Cover with sauce, then polenta rectangles, and then cheese. Repeat with one more layer, ending with the cheese.

Bake for 25 minutes, until the cheese is melted and the dish is hot. Serve hot with crusty bread and a big green salad topped with garbanzo beans.

Tempeh and Wild Mushroom Stew

Serves 4

*T*empeh *is a great way to get soy and is even better for you than tofu. Combined with mushrooms, it is a real winner. Steaming the tempeh opens it up to absorbing more flavor. You can also make it without the tempeh and if you love mushrooms, as I do, it is still delicious.*

1-2	**ounces dried mushrooms such as porcini, morel or shiitake**
1	**cup water plus 1/2 cup water**
8	**ounces tempeh, cut into cubes**
1	**pound wild and regular mushrooms, any combination is fine**
1	**large red onion, chopped**
2-3	**teaspoons miso or wild mushroom broth**
1	**tablespoon arrowroot**
1	**tablespoon fresh rosemary, chopped, or 1 teaspoon crumbled dried rosemary**

Freshly ground black pepper and salt, to taste

Boil the cup of water and soak the dried mushrooms, if they are morels or shiitake, for 30 minutes. Save the clean soaking water. If using porcini, add when recommended.

Steam the tempeh over boiling water for 15 minutes. Remove from heat and let cool.

Heat the sauté pan over medium heat. Add the onion and sauté for 3 to 5 minutes, until it starts to soften. Add the chopped wild mushroom, the tempeh cubes and rosemary. Cook for about 7-8 minutes.

Add the mushroom soaking water, drained of any debris or dirt, and the porcini, if using them. Add the miso or mushroom broth and stir. Cook for another couple of minutes until the mushrooms are mostly cooked.

Combine the remaining 1/2 cup water with the arrowroot. Remove the pan from the heat, stir in the arrowroot mixture until well combined and then put back on the heat. If the mixture is too thick, add water 1 tablespoon at a time. If too thin, cook down or add 1 teaspoon arrowroot mixed with 1 tablespoon water until desired consistency. Season with black pepper. Add salt to taste.

Serve hot over noodles, rice, quinoa, barley or other grain.

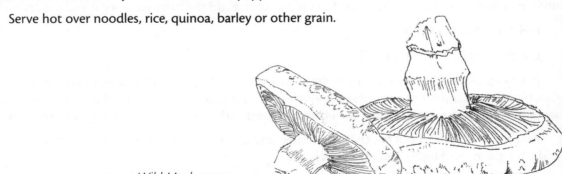

Wild Mushrooms

The Veggie Queen™: Vegetables Get The Royal Treatment

Pasta with Romanesco Broccoli, Capers and Sun Dried Tomatoes

Serves 4-6

The light green and red colors and bright flavors in this recipe lighten up any winter day. If you follow McDougall, cut the oil at the beginning and dry sauté. Add 2-3 tablespoons additional vegetable broth to give a saucier consistency.

2	tablespoons olive oil
1/2	medium onion, diced
2	cloves garlic, minced
4	cups Romanesco broccoli florets
6-8	sundried tomatoes, rehydrated and cut into slivers
1	teaspoon crushed red pepper
1/4	cup or more vegetable broth
2	tablespoons capers, rinsed
3/4	pound whole grain pasta, cooked according to directions until al dente
2-3	teaspoons Meyer or other lemon juice
2	tablespoons chopped Italian parsley

Grated soy Parmesan cheese, to taste

Heat 1 tablespoon of the olive oil in a skillet over medium heat. Add the onion and sauté for 5 minutes, stirring occasionally. Add the garlic and broccoli florets. Sauté for 5 more minutes. Add the tomatoes and red pepper and the vegetable broth. Cook until the broccoli is tender but not mushy, about 8-10 minutes, adding broth only if the pan gets too dry. When pasta is cooked and drained, add it to the pan with the broccoli. Add the capers, the remaining tablespoon of olive oil, a squeeze of lemon juice and stir to combine. Top the pasta with Italian parsley and grated cheese. Serve hot.

Romanesco Broccoli

Winter Squash Enchiladas

Serves 4-6

only recently began making enchiladas at my son's request. Since then I have developed a number of terrific seasonal stuffing recipes. This one is perfect for winter with the abundance of squash. Enchilada sauce is something that tastes fine canned; it's hardly worth the effort making it.

1	package of 12 corn tortillas, yellow or white
	canola oil
1	28 oz. can enchilada sauce
1	tablespoon canola oil
1	medium onion, diced
1	red Anaheim or other medium-hot pepper, seeded and diced
2	cloves garlic, minced to equal 1 tablespoon
8	ounces firm tofu, diced small
2	pounds kabocha, delicata or butternut squash, peeled and cut into 1/2-1 inch dice
1	tablespoon ground cumin
1	chipotle pepper, rehydrated, seeded and diced
1/2	cup fresh or frozen, thawed corn
1	teaspoon salt
2-3	tablespoons chopped fresh cilantro
	Tofu sour cream for garnish

Spray a large glass baking dish with cooking spray or oil.

Add the canola oil to a large skillet over medium heat. Add the onion and pepper and sauté for 5 minutes. Add the garlic, tofu, squash, cumin and chipotle pepper. Cook for 5 minutes, stirring occasionally. Cover the skillet and let cook for 5 more minutes. Stir to turn bottom to top. Add the corn and cover again. Continue the stirring and covering process until the squash is cooked through, in 15 to 20 minutes. Add the salt. Let cool a bit and add the cilantro and cheese.

While the squash is cooking, heat a nonstick skillet over medium high heat. Spray with cooking spray or lightly coat with oil. Add the tortillas, one at a time, flipping from one side to another after 15 seconds. As you remove each tortilla, dip it in enchilada sauce. Fill with 1/4 to 1/3 cup filling and roll. Place seam side down in the baking sheet. Lightly drizzle the enchilada sauce over the entire dish. Cover and bake for 20 minutes, or until heated through.

Garnish with tofu sour cream, if desired. Sprinkle with more cilantro if you like.

Winter Squash Tips

I think that the reason that more people don't eat winter squash is because cutting them open can seem so daunting. And I will tell you that more than once I have stood at my kitchen counter with my knife impaled in a squash, neither going in more nor coming out. A few sharp whacks on the counter usually loosens the knife, at which point I jump back to be sure that all my limbs and digits stay intact.

To avoid this scenario, I suggest that you get yourself a pumpkin carving knife. You can get the dull kind that little kids use or the sharper kind for adults. Either will work for many types of squash. Just insert the knife and use a sawing action to cut it open. If it still seems too hard, you can put the squash into the microwave in a dish and nuke it for a couple of minutes. This will soften the squash a bit and make it easier to cut.

One of my class participants suggested baking the squash whole but I don't like leaving the innards inside as I think that it sometimes taints the flavor and texture of your squash. Certainly, it's up to you.

Storing squash is easy. The ideal place is in your root cellar. What? You don't have one? OK, neither do I. So, the next best place is somewhere dark and cool such as your garage or basement. Refrigerator storage is not recommended. Winter squash can be stored for up to 6 months or more. When they get moldy or hollow, throw them out. Since I also use them as a centerpiece and they are in the light, mine usually last for 3 to 4 months. But the benefit of seeing them is that it's a reminder to eat them.

My favorite way to cook squash is simply. I carefully cut it in half, usually from top to bottom or stem to butt end. I place the halves cut side down in a glass baking dish with 1 inch of water and roast at 400° for 15 minutes. Then I turn the squash and continue roasting until the squash is soft. Delicata, my favorite squash, only takes about 15 to 30 minutes. I then scoop out the flesh with a spoon and make it into soup, custard or pie or eat it as is. Yummy.

Squash

You don't have to cook fancy or complicated masterpieces - just good food from fresh ingredients.

Julia Child,
Cooking Grande Dame and cookbook author (1912 - 2004)

Anytime
At All

*S*ome recipes defy categorization, either because they are items such as salad dressings or burgers that you might use any day or they are dishes that are easily adapted to one season or another like quinoa, a basic grain dish. Some may become staples in your diet. Anything that transcends the seasons is found here.

Rice Paper Rolls with Spicy Citrus Sauce

Makes 18 rolls

*T*his is always a hit with guests. You can use anything that you like for the filling. You can make them earlier in the day; wrap them well in plastic and refrigerate them.

8-12 ounces of baked tofu, cut into thin strips
1 1/2 cups mung bean or sunflower sprouts
4 green onions, chopped
2 tablespoons chopped fresh mint
1 tablespoon Bragg's liquid amino acids
1 tablespoon fresh lime juice
1 large red pepper, cut into thin strips or
   2 carrots cut into strips and steamed lightly
18 8-inch rice papers

Spicy Citrus Sauce:

3 tablespoons orange juice
2 tablespoons lime juice
1 tablespoon reduced-sodium tamari or soy sauce
1 tablespoon rice wine vinegar
1 tablespoon toasted sesame oil
1 tablespoon chili paste with garlic
1 tablespoon finely chopped green onions
2 teaspoons honey or maple syrup
2 tablespoons chopped roasted peanuts

Spicy Citrus Sauce:

Mix all ingredients together in a bowl or shake in a jar. This sauce will keep for a few days.

For a pretty touch, tie a strip of blanched green onion around each packet.

In a bowl, combine the sprouts, green onions, mint, Bragg's and lime juice. (The filling can be made up to 4 hours ahead and stored, covered, in the refrigerator.)

In a pie plate or large bowl of very warm water, soak one rice paper until it is softened, about 30 seconds. Place it on a clean dish towel. Slide the next wrapper in while you fill the first.

Put a few strips of tofu, red pepper and sprout filling in the center of each rice paper and fold in the side edges of the rice paper. Fold the edge closest to you up and then roll like a burrito. Repeat with the remaining rice papers and filling. (The packets can be made up to 2 hours ahead; wrap them in a damp kitchen towel, place them in a plastic bag and store them in the refrigerator or a cooler.)

Serve with a small bowl of Spicy Citrus Sauce for dipping. days.

Inspiration

Sometimes when I eat a new dish I feel like I just have to learn how to make it. This is what happened the first time that I ate Vietnamese Spring Rolls (also called Rice Paper Wrapped Rolls) in a restaurant. Immediately I dissected what went into the dish so I could replicate it.

First I needed to find a source for the rice wrappers. Since I lived in Los Angeles that was easy. I went to the Asian grocery. (They are also now available at some natural food stores.) But I had no idea how to actually rehydrate them. A little experimentation led me to find that it worked best to slide the thin, brittle wrappers into a large glass pie plate of warm water for about 30 seconds. They were then pliable and ready to use. I put the wrapper on a clean countertop and partially covered it with a leaf of butter lettuce. I then added thin strips of red pepper, mint, cilantro, baked tofu and wrapped it like a burrito.

Since then I have come up with a multitude of fillings for the wrappers, all of which taste good to me. I vary the sauce, too, which is usually sweet and spicy. Occasionally it contains peanuts or citrus juice. It just depends upon my mood. But it's the chewy texture of the rice paper wrappers that makes this dish work for me.

Hummus

Makes 1 3/4 cups   Will serve 6 as an appetizer

*N*o vegetarian book would be complete without a recipe for hummus. It's easily adaptable and easy to make. Using canned beans makes it as quick as a trip to the store. Why buy it at the store when you can flavor any way that you like at home? It's a great dip or sandwich spread and can be made into salad dressing. At least that's what one of my students told me.

This is good served with warmed pita bread triangles or raw vegetables. Sometimes I put it in pita bread with salad and eat it for a sandwich.

2	cloves garlic
1 1/2 -2	cups cooked garbanzo beans, you may use canned
2	tablespoons sesame tahini
2	tablespoons fresh lemon juice
1/2	teaspoon ground cumin (optional)
1	dash of cayenne pepper
1	tablespoon reduced sodium tamari or Bragg's liquid amino acids
2 to 4 tablespoons water	

Put garlic in food processor to be sure that it gets well chopped. Whir for about 15 seconds. Add the remaining ingredients, blending until it's the desired consistency. If it seems too thick, add more water or lemon juice.

Garlic

Crostini

Makes about 40 toasts

If you need to dissipate your nervous energy, cutting bread can help. This is an easy contribution to an impromptu gathering. Some bakeries have a slicing machine that can cut your baguettes. If you don't want to use the oil you can just rub the cut bread with the garlic and bake it. The toasts are still tasty, especially after you put on a delicious topping.

1	**8 ounce baguette**
1-2	**tablespoons olive oil (optional)**
1-2	**cloves garlic, cut in half**

Preheat oven to 350 degrees F.

Using a serrated knife, cut the baguette into about 40 slices. Place on baking sheet and, using a pastry brush, lightly coat each slice with olive oil, if using, and rub with the cut side of the garlic clove.

Bake for 5 minutes. Then turn and brush the other side with oil. Bake 5 more minutes. (You can brush both sides of the bread before putting them in the oven if you'd like.) Let cool and serve with Mediterranean Greens (page??), hummus or other favorite topping.

These will last 1 week in the refrigerator or a couple of days without refrigeration.

Creamy Roasted Red Pepper Dressing

Makes 2 cups

Fresh basil really enhances the flavor of this brightly colored dressing. If you must use dried, then use only a couple of tablespoons. If you can't buy it, you may want to grow your own. This can be stored at least 4 days in the refrigerator, if you haven't used it up before then.

1/2	**box Mori Nu lite firm tofu**
2/3	**cup roasted red pepper, chopped**
1	**cup green onions, chopped (green part only)**
2	**cloves garlic, chopped**
1/2	**cup water**
2	**tablespoons each orange juice and red wine or other vinegar**
2	**tablespoons packed basil leaves, freshly chopped**
2	**teaspoons Braggs liquid Amino Acids or 1/4 teaspoon salt**
1/4- 1/2	**teaspoon freshly ground black pepper**

Put everything into a blender and blend well. If the mixture is too thick, add some more liquid of your choice. Taste and adjust seasonings. Serve over green salad, potatoes, grains or other vegetables.

Caesary Salad Dressing

Serves 4

I have many variations on this salad dressing recipe and I like them all. I think it's all the garlic that makes it taste great. Someone said that I ought to be called the "Garlic Queen."

4	cloves garlic, minced or pressed
1/2	box Mori Nu lite silken tofu
2-3	tablespoons Dijon mustard
3-4	tablespoons nutritional yeast flakes
2	tablespoons tamari, Bragg's liquid amino acids or soy sauce
3	tablespoons lemon juice
2	tablespoons or more water, depending upon consistency you like

Finely chop the garlic in a food processor until it is in small pieces. Add the remaining ingredients and process until smooth. Refrigerate until serving time. (Will last for 1 week in the refrigerator.)

Note: *You can make this in the blender but you need to mince the garlic by hand before adding it.*

Zesty Lemon Garlic Dressing

Makes about 1 cup

This dressing tastes great on salad, of course, but also on baked potatoes, broccoli and asparagus, as a dip for artichokes or even on cooked pasta, if you dare. It can also be used as a dip.

To zest a lemon, you either need to use a zester, a Microplane™ or regular grater. Be sure to only use the colored part of the lemon. The pith underneath is bitter.

1	box Mori Nu silken lite firm tofu
1	lemon, zested and juiced to equal 3 tablespoons
2	cloves garlic, crushed or minced
1/2	teaspoon black pepper
1/2	teaspoon salt
1/2	cup vegetable stock or vegetable broth powder and water
1/2	teaspoon Sucanat or other sweetener
1	tablespoon extra virgin olive oil

Combine all ingredients in a blender or food processor until smooth. Taste and add lemon juice, garlic or salt to taste.

Rice and Veggie Sushi Salad

Serves 4 to 6

I *nspired by a recipe in Moosewood Restaurant Lowfat Favorites, this recipe was one of the winners in John Ash's Good Food Hour rice recipe contest sponsored by KSRO, my local radio station. John said that he loved the clean flavors. I like it because it tastes like sushi, only better, since I can add many vegetables. I use brown, not sushi, rice because I like the texture better.*

1	cup short grain brown rice
1 1/2	cups water
1/4	cup rice vinegar
2	tablespoons ume plum vinegar
2	tablespoons Sucanat or sugar
2	teaspoons grated fresh ginger
1	teaspoon wasabi powder and 1 teaspoon water
2	medium carrots, peeled and diced
1	cup fresh or frozen, thawed green soybeans, also called edamame
1/2	cup diced daikon radish
1	cup mung bean sprouts
1/4	cup sliced green onions
1	ripe avocado, cut into chunks
1	sheet toasted nori seaweed
2	tablespoons black or brown sesame seeds, toasted

Washed Asian greens, like mizuna, tatsoi or red mustard

Bring the water to a boil in a medium saucepan. Stir in the rice. Cover and reduce the heat to a simmer. Cook for 40 minutes, then remove from the heat and let stand for 10 minutes.

While the rice is cooking blanch the carrots and sweet beans in boiling water or steam for 2-3 minutes.

In a nonreactive bowl, such as glass or stainless steel, combine the rice vinegar, ume vinegar, Sucanat, ginger and wasabi.

Tear the nori sheet into small strips and combine with the sesame seeds.

In a large bowl, combine the cooked warm rice with the vinegar sauce and the vegetables, except the avocado. When ready to serve, carefully combine the avocado. Sprinkle the rice mixture with the nori-sesame mixture. Put the greens on plates and serve the rice salad on top.

Note: *When other vegetables are in season, such as cucumber, red pepper, peas or summer squash, use them in this salad. Also, you can mix in any leftover cooked vegetables such as green beans or broccoli florets.*

Oil Substitute for Salad Dressing

Makes 1 cup

This recipe is especially for those following the McDougall diet but it works well for anyone who wants to decrease the fat in their salad dressings.

It is almost identical to a recipe by Bryana Clark Grogan in The (Almost) No Fat Cookbook, The Book Publishing Company.

Mix together in a small saucepan:

1	cup water or vegetarian broth
1	tablespoon cornstarch

Cook, stirring constantly, over high heat until thickened and clear. Let cool.

Use this in place of oil in your favorite dressings (it will thicken further when chilled).

Daikon Delight

I love eating green salad. But in the winter it is often difficult to get excited about the limited scope of seasonal ingredients going into the bowl. That's why when I see something colorful, new and interesting, I buy it and try it.

One day while shopping at Community Market, my local natural foods store, I saw a pale green, pink-tinged globe the size of a baseball that had been cut in half. The inside was bright fuschia. It was called either a watermelon radish or daikon. Having eaten traditional white daikon, a long and cylindrical foot-long root, I thought that perhaps I would like the flavor, which is usually milder than traditional red radishes that do not agree with me. Most of all I yearned for color in my winter salad bowl.

Well, it turned out that this daikon has an even sweeter flavor than the white variety. Unfortunately, the pink variety is not readily available. Imagine how lucky I felt to find a bunch of five of these tasty treats for $1.50 at the farmer's market the week between Christmas and New Year's Eve. What a bright start for the New Year.

I was lured to the farmer's market the next week with the anticipation of collecting another bunch of watermelon daikon and placing it in my canvas bag. Unfortunately the grower didn't have them. But all was not lost, for I headed to Community Market where I had first purchased them. In a small bin, tucked toward the back of the produce section, I found gems that my salad needed. I had to pay almost twice the price, but for their gorgeous color alone they are worth it.

If you want to avoid daikon disappointment, I suggest that you grow them yourself as my friend Jon did since he loved them so. If you're not a gardener, just buy them when you see them. And if it is whole, insist on having the produce person cut it open for a peek at its color. Then have a taste. No doubt watermelon radish or daikon will become one of your winter favorites, too.

Chinese "No-Chicken" Salad

Serves 4 to 6

*A*t one time this type of salad was very popular. It still tastes great. Instead of baked tofu you could use one of the refrigerated vegetarian chicken substitutes made from soy or gluten, which didn't exist when I wrote this recipe. The flavors are vibrant. It's a hit at potluck dinners.

1	package baked Ramen Soup mix - get one of the "healthy" ones such as Westbrae or Soken
2	tablespoons reduced sodium tamari
4	tablespoons rice vinegar
2	teaspoons sesame oil
1	tablespoon honey or other sweetener
1	tablespoon grated ginger
6	cups cabbage, cut thinly into shreds
3 to 4	green onions, chopped
8	ounces baked tofu
4	tablespoons chopped cilantro
2	tablespoons sesame seeds, toasted

Mix the small packet of soup flavoring mix with the tamari, vinegar, oil and honey. Shake well. Break the soup noodles into pieces in a large bowl. Combine the dressing mixture with the noodles and remaining ingredients, reserving sesame seeds and 1 tablespoon chopped cilantro for garnish. Let sit in the refrigerator for about an hour. Toss the mixture, top with sesame seeds and cilantro, and serve.

Asian Slaw

Serves 6

*T*his slaw doesn't have a creamy dressing but it has plenty of flavor from the green onions and cilantro. If you want it spicier add a pinch of chipotle powder, cayenne or a bit of jalapeno pepper. You can use this for the filling for Rice Paper Rolls, page 88.

3-4	cups thinly sliced green cabbage
1	teaspoon sea salt
1	cup grated carrot
1/4	cup finely sliced green onions, both white and green parts
2	tablespoons rice wine vinegar
2	teaspoons canola oil
1	teaspoon toasted sesame oil
1/2-1	teaspoon Sucanat
1/4	cup chopped cilantro
2	tablespoons sesame seeds, toasted
Freshly grated black pepper, to taste	

Combine the cabbage and sea salt in a large bowl. Get a plate that fits into the bowl and weight down the plate. Let sit on countertop for 20 to 30 minutes. Then squeeze the liquid out of the cabbage.

Combine the cabbage with the carrot, green onions, rice vinegar, canola and sesame oils and Sucanat, stirring well. Refrigerate for at least 20 minutes. Then stir in cilantro, sesame seeds and black pepper. Serve chilled or at room temperature.

Note: *If you want this to taste more like traditional cole slaw, use a tofu or mayonnaise based dressing.*

Creamy Spinach Soup

Serves 4

*T*his could just as easily be Creamy Anything Soup. I have made it with almost every vegetable and it's delicious each time. The seasoning will vary according to the vegetable. Experiment and have fun. The basics are always the onion, tofu, soy or other milk, potatoes and water and broth powder (or broth or stock instead of the latter two ingredients).

1	**bunch spinach, washed and chopped or 1 10 oz package frozen chopped spinach, thawed**
1/2	**medium onion, chopped**
1/2	**box Mori Nu firm silken tofu or 6 oz other**
1/2	**cup soy or other milk**
2	**small potatoes**
3	**tablespoons chicken-flavored broth powder**
2 3/4	**cups water**
2	**tablespoons parsley, chopped**
1	**tablespoon parsley or chives and their flowers, for garnish**

Salt and pepper to taste

Onions

Cut potatoes into quarters. Combine broth powder and water in a saucepan. Add potatoes and onion and cook until almost tender, about 10 minutes. Stir in the spinach. Remove 1 cup of this mixture and set aside.

Puree the tofu and soy milk in the food processor until perfectly creamy.

Using a hand blender, if you have one, puree the mixture in the pot until almost smooth. (If you don't have a hand blender, use a blender, very carefully or a food processor to blend.) Add parsley at the end of pureeing. Mix in the tofu puree.

Heat gently, but do not allow to boil or the tofu mixture will curdle. Season with salt and pepper. Garnish with parsley or chives and their flowers.

Note: This soup adapts well to almost any vegetable. Give it a whirl. I've made it with carrots, asparagus, mushrooms, corn and more. Use 1 1/2 to 2 cups of vegetables. I've not yet been able to add too many vegetables to this soup. If it seems too thick, thin it with broth, water or nondairy milk. Adjust the seasonings and enjoy.

One Onion

As a recipe writer I find it difficult to decide whether to ask you to dice one medium onion, or to use 1 cup of diced onion since I don't know the real size of your medium onion. If I recommend 1 cup of onion you may wonder what to do with the 1/4 cup remaining. Don't worry about it.

Onions are one of my favorite vegetables. How about you? If you like them too, please realize most recipes won't be ruined by a little additional onion. So, relax and have fun cooking rather than worrying about the size of your onion.

On the other hand when it comes to peppers, especially hot ones, you may want to use exactly what the recipe calls for, unless you are a hothead like I am. But that's another topic.

Basic Quinoa

Serves 4

Q uinoa must be rinsed under water in a fine
mesh strainer to remove a natural soapy
substance called saponin, which can make it taste
bitter. Quinoa tastes great hot and makes a terrific
side dish, and it's just as tasty the next day made
into a salad.

1/2   onion, diced
1   cup quinoa, rinsed well
1 3/4 cups water or broth
Salt and pepper to taste

Heat a saucepan with a tight-fitting lid over
medium heat. Put in the onion and sauté for a
few minutes. Stir in the quinoa and toast it for
1-2 minutes. Add the water or broth. Bring to
a boil, then reduce the heat to a simmer. Cover
and cook for 12 minutes. Remove from the
heat, leaving it covered, and let sit for 5
minutes. Remove cover. Fluff and add salt and
pepper to taste. Serve hot.

Notes: I cook quinoa many different ways.
In my Asian style quinoa, I add ginger and
garlic when cooking the quinoa for the 12
minutes. When it has 5 minutes left to cook I
add broccoli florets to the pan and leave them
covered for 5 minutes. Once removed from
the heat, I add tamari and a bit of sesame oil.
After fluffing the grains I top them with
toasted sesame seeds.

For Quinoa with Sun Dried Tomatoes and
Pine Nuts, I add garlic and diced sundried
tomatoes to the basic recipe. After the quinoa
is cooked, I stir in fresh basil and Italian parsley
and then top with pine nuts. Or I might make
Quinoa with Pistachios to which I add curry
powder when cooking, and green onions and
chopped roasted pistachios for a garnish.

Quinoa is incredibly versatile: use your
favorite seasonings and ingredients when
cooking. The next day it can be turned into a
salad with the addition of a light dressing and
cooked veggies or beans.

Grain Cooking Tips

I am not sure why, but it's important when
you cook more than one cup of grain to use
less than double the amount of water for the
subsequent cups of grain cooked. (I use a
similar formula when adding salt to recipes so
that they don't end up too salty.) For the
second cup of grain, I usually use 1/4 cup less
water and on like that, always using just a bit
less liquid each time I add another cup of grain.
For instance, to cook one cup of quinoa, use 1
3/4 cups water and one cup of grain. If you have
two cups quinoa to cook, use 1 3/4 cups plus 1
1/2 cups for a total of 3 1/4 cups water. If the
math has you stymied, just double the water
and have your slotted spoon handy to remove
any excess liquid.

The Veggie Queen™: Vegetables Get The Royal Treatment

Rich Mushroom Gravy

Makes 3 cups

*T*his is great served with mashed potatoes. See Page 116 for a great mashed potato recipe. You can also serve this alongside stuffing at the holidays, or any day that you want to feel like a holiday. You make this recipe without the oil by dry sautéing the mushrooms and then setting them aside. Be sure to brown the flour well for a rich taste without the added oil.

2   **tablespoons oil**
6   **ounces crimini mushrooms, thinly sliced**
1   **cup spelt flour**
1/2   **teaspoon thyme**
1/2   **teaspoon black pepper**
3   **cups water**
1/4   **cup reduced sodium tamari**
2   **teaspoons lemon juice**
2 to 3 **tablespoons nutritional yeast**

In a saucepan, heat the oil over medium heat. Add the mushrooms and sauté for 5 minutes, until they start to brown and release a bit of liquid. Remove the mushrooms and set aside. Add the flour, thyme and pepper to the pan and stir constantly until the flour is lightly toasted. Gradually add water with a whisk. When blended, add the mushrooms and the last 3 ingredients and mix well. Adjust the seasonings as needed. You can add a little bit of sugar or maple syrup for balance. Serve hot.

Variation: Soak 1/2 ounce dried mushrooms (such as porcini or shiitake) in 1 cup warm or hot water for 30 minutes. Use part of this soaking water (the part without dirt and debris) as the liquid for the gravy. Finely chop the drained, soaked mushrooms and add to gravy mixture before adding the last 3 ingredients.

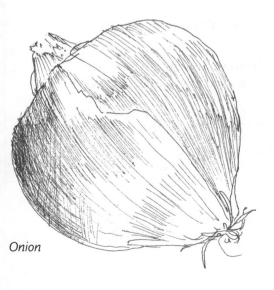

Onion

Mushroom Oat Burgers

Serves 4

*V*egetables form the basis of this burger. The oats give them a nice crunch. They are similar to a popular commercially prepared veggie burger.

Vegetable cooking spray
1   **cup chopped onion**
1/3   **pound mushrooms. sliced to equal about 1 1/2 cups**
1/2   **cup chopped broccoli**
1   **medium carrot, grated to equal 1/2 cup**
3   **cloves garlic, minced**
1/4   **cup chopped roasted red pepper**
3/4   **cup cooked brown rice**
1   **tablespoon egg replacer mixed with 1/4 cup water or 2 egg whites**
1/2   **cup grated soy or mozzarella cheese**
1 3/4 **cups rolled oats, divided**
1/2   **teaspoon pepper**
Salt to taste

Spray a nonstick sauté pan with cooking spray. Add onion and cook over medium heat for 3 minutes. Add the mushrooms, broccoli, carrot and garlic and sauté for another 2 minutes. Cover pan and cook for another 5 minutes. Remove from heat and put vegetable mixture in a medium bowl. Rinse pan for later use.

Let vegetables cool slightly, and put in a food processor with roasted red pepper, brown rice and egg replacer mixture or egg whites. Process for 15 to 30 seconds until the mixture still has some texture but no large chunks. Add the cheese and 1 cup of the oats and process for another 10 seconds, pulsing on and off. Empty processor contents into a large bowl and combine with the remaining oats, salt and pepper, stirring thoroughly.

The burger mixture will be a bit wet, but will firm up considerably with cooking. Form into 8 patties 3-inches in diameter and 3/4-inch thick.

Spray the pan with cooking spray. Add the patties to the pan and cook over medium heat for 5 minutes. Flip burgers and cook 5 more minutes. Serve on buns with traditional toppings.

Note: *After cooking, these burgers may be refrigerated or frozen and thawed. They can then be warmed through in a toaster oven or on the grill.*

Herbed Lentil Burgers

Serves 6

Y*ou can't have too many burger recipes. Find the ones that you like and make extra to freeze. Then you can pretend that you went out and bought them for a quick and easy lunch or dinner.*

1	cup cooked lentils
2	tablespoons reduced sodium tamari
1/2	cup chopped tomatoes
1	cup grated carrots
1/2	cup textured vegetable protein (TVP)
2	tablespoons peanut butter
1	clove garlic, pressed
1/3	cup finely chopped onion
1/2	teaspoon dried sage
1/2	teaspoon dried thyme
2	tablespoons chopped fresh parsley
1	tablespoon canola, olive or vegetable oil
1/4	cup whole wheat pastry flour

Vegetable cooking spray

Combine lentils and tamari in food processor. Remove from processor and mix well with remaining ingredients, except oil, flour and cooking spray. Let rest for 15 minutes. Return to food processor and process for about 15 seconds. Shape into 6 patties. Lightly flour each side of the burger before cooking.

Spray a pan with cooking spray. Add oil over medium heat and cook patties until browned, about 5 minutes. Spray the top side of burger with cooking spray before turning. Brown on second side.

Mushroom Veggie Burgers

Serves 6

I *like this burger recipe because I love eating mushrooms and the ingredient list is short.*

1	tablespoon oil
1/2	cup finely diced onion
1/2	pound mushrooms, shiitake, crimini or Portabello, sliced
3	cloves garlic, minced
4	cups spinach leaves, washed
5	sundried tomatoes, rehydrated in boiling water, chopped fine
1	cup cooked bulgur, rice or quinoa

1-1/2 cups bread crumbs
Salt and pepper

Heat oil in a large skillet or sauté pan. Add the onion and sauté for about 1 minute over medium heat. Add the mushrooms and cook for 3 to 4 minutes. Add the garlic, sauté 1 minute more. Then lay the spinach on top of the vegetable mixture. Cover and let spinach wilt for 1 to 2 minutes. Put this mixture into the processor and whir until mixed. Add the bulgur and pulse to combine. Put mixture into a bowl. Add the sundried tomatoes, breadcrumbs and salt and pepper. Mix with a spoon or your hands until everything is combined. Form into 6 patties about 3-inches in diameter and 1/2 inch thick. Pan fry or grill for 5 to 8 minutes per side or until lightly browned.

Baked Tofu

Makes 4 servings

*B*aking tofu changes the texture, making it firmer, drier and more acceptable to many people. The joy of doing it yourself is that you don't have to use any oil, if you don't want to, and you can season it any way that you prefer.

1	**pound vacuum-packed extra firm or firm tofu**
3	**tablespoons rice vinegar**
2	**tablespoons reduced sodium tamari**
2	**teaspoons sesame oil (optional)**
2	**cloves garlic, minced**
1	**tablespoon of your favorite herb or spice blend** (*I especially like mole rub or Berber spice-which are both available on my website www.theveggiequeen.com, but five-spice or an Italian herb blend works well, too.*)

Preheat oven to 400 degrees F.

Slice the tofu into 4 pieces or more depending upon how you slice it. I like to slice it horizontally so that the slices are large rectangles. But how you cut it is up to you.

Lay the tofu slices in a large glass baking dish. Mix the rice vinegar, tamari and oil and pour over the sliced tofu. Tilt the dish a bit so the marinade spreads. Sprinkle the garlic and herbs or spices over the tofu. Let marinate for at least 15 minutes. (If you choose to marinate it for longer than an hour, you must do this in the refrigerator.) Turn the tofu over and place in the oven.

Bake for 15 minutes. Turn the tofu and bake another 5 to 10 minutes until the marinade in the pan and the tofu pieces are dry. Let the tofu sit in the pan for 5 minutes before removing.

This can be eaten as-is or used in sandwiches, stir-fries, salads and other recipes.

About serving sizes

When my recipes say that the serving size is for 4 to 6, especially for salads, that means that not everyone eats as much salad as I do. In fact, I suspect that most people do not eat nearly as much salad as I do. Most of my recipes that serve 4 to 6 are designed for "average" eaters. Do you know any? If you like to eat large servings, then judge how many the recipe will serve accordingly. I have tried to be accurate when listing serving sizes, erring on the side of having leftovers rather than being caught short.

If you look at the salad and it appears that there's too much to eat that night, then I recommend that you don't dress it all. Most green salads will not hold up after they have been dressed. On the other hand, pasta, potato and grain-based salads may actually taste better after they have absorbed some of the dressing.

When it comes to green leafy vegetables because they are so nutrition-packed, it would be hard to eat too many in terms of calories or health. Feel free to splurge on these. However, it's probably best to watch the portion sizes of grain- or other starch-based dishes if you are concerned about your weight. One can even gain weight eating so-called "good for you" food. It's really all about the portion size. The serving sizes that you see are my best estimate.

Curried Lentils and Rice

Serves 4

*T*his recipe is highly adaptable. You can add other vegetables to it while it is cooking, or at the end. Stir in chopped spinach at the end of cooking, if you like, or add potatoes to the pot at the beginning. This is really good wrapped in a whole grain tortilla. And it's great for a hearty breakfast.

2	teaspoons canola or vegetable oil
1 1/2	cups onion, chopped
2	slices ginger, finely minced to equal about 1 teaspoon
2	cloves of garlic, finely minced
1	small hot pepper, finely minced
1	cup brown or green lentils, rinsed and drained
1/2	cup basmati or other long grain rice
2 3/4	cups water or broth
1	tablespoon curry powder
1/2-1	teaspoon salt
1	cup frozen peas, defrosted
1	cup diced tomatoes, fresh or canned
3-4	tablespoons chopped cilantro, for garnish

Hot sauce or chutney, to taste

    Pour the oil into a medium or large saucepan with a lid over medium heat. Add the onion, ginger, garlic and pepper. Sauté for 1 to 2 minutes. Cook until onion begins to slightly soften, about 5 minutes. Add lentils, rice, curry powder, and water. Stir well. Cover the pan and bring to a boil. Reduce heat to low and simmer for 35 minutes. Remove from heat, add peas to pot, replace cover and let sit undisturbed for 5 more minutes. Add tomatoes and salt and fluff with a fork. Transfer to a serving plate. Top with cilantro. Serve immediately.

Seasonal Sweet and Sour Veggie Stir-Fry

Serves 4

*M*ake this with the freshest available vegetables. I almost always have carrots, onion and broccoli around, yet I have also made it with cauliflower or Romanesco broccoli in the winter. In the summer I use many varieties of squash or green beans. It's easiest to control the timing if you stick to no more than 4 vegetables. Add tofu, tempeh or seitan to make this a quick and easy main dish.

2	teaspoons oil (optional)
1	piece ginger 1/2 to 1-inch long, peeled and minced
2	carrots cut on diagonal
1	medium onion, sliced lengthwise
3	cups broccoli florets
2	cloves garlic, minced
3	tablespoons reduced sodium tamari, divided
1	tablespoon rice or cider vinegar
1	tablespoon Sucanat, sugar or a few drops of stevia liquid
2	tablespoons water or vegetable broth
1	tablespoon arrowroot or cornstarch
2	green onions, chopped for garnish

Sesame seeds, for garnish (optional)

Place a wok or large sauté pan over medium high heat. Add oil, if using, and ginger. Let this cook for 1 minute, then add carrots and stir-fry for 2 minutes, adding water or stock, a teaspoon at a time, if they begin to stick. Add the onion and stir-fry until the onion turns translucent, about 5 minutes. Add broccoli and garlic and stir-fry with 1 tablespoon reduced sodium tamari. Whisk remaining tamari, vinegar, Sucanat, water or broth and arrowroot or cornstarch in a small bowl. Remove pan from the heat, pour in the tamari mixture and stir well. Put the pan back on low heat and cook until sauce begins to thicken. Remove from the heat and transfer to a serving dish containing quinoa, rice or noodles. Sprinkle with green onions and sesame seeds.

Lovely Legumes

Full of Beans

Beans, peas and lentils have leapt from peasant fare to upscale, found at expensive restaurants and gourmet stores. The range of available legumes, which is what they are called, is amazing. You'll find tiny black Beluga lentils, just a fraction of an inch round, to Christmas lima or scarlet runner beans, at a full inch or two long. Each legume looks different and can be used in a myriad of recipes from appetizers through dessert.

I praise beans for their versatility and variety, however their taste holds the allure. If you've tried limas and didn't like them (most people say they don't), then try garbanzo, also known as chickpea, or kidney beans, or green (edamame), yellow or black soybeans. The range of colors seen in beans is astounding.

Beans that have been in existence for a long time are called "heirloom" beans. While grown from "old" stock, they are usually more recently harvested. Old beans will not completely cook through and are often tough. Buying beans at a natural food store rather than in a bag at the supermarket will usually yield a newer crop of beans. And a specialty bean purveyor will have the freshest (see Sources).

Tierra Vegetables' farm stand in Santa Rosa, California sells a bean called Marrow Fat. It's so creamy and delicious that it has been added to the Slow Foods Ark, to be preserved for future generations.

Just a sampling of other terrific tasting heirlooms includes Anasazi, borlotti, flageolet, Jacob's cattle, and yellow eye Stueben. There are so many legume varieties to explore that you could try one a week for a year or more.

Eating beans often seems to help your body adjust to beans and decreases gas. If that doesn't work, you can try a product called Beano. Or try adding kombu seaweed when cooking beans. Do not add salt or other acidic foods such as tomatoes or molasses during cooking or else your beans may be tough. To boost flavor, add herbs, spices or garlic to your bean pot.

There's an old saying, "Beans, beans, good for your heart..." Protect your heart today in a tasty way.

Here are a few important tips for cooking beans:

Do NOT add salt or acid foods such as tomatoes or molasses when cooking beans.

Adding seasonings while cooking beans infuses them with flavor.

Use them for soups, salads or main dishes.

Freeze what you don't use for later use.

"Nothing will benefit human health and increase chances for survival of life on Earth as much as the evolution to a vegetarian diet."

Albert Einstein,
Scientist, (1879-1955)

Pressure's on
In a Good Way

Whenever I mention that I teach pressure cooking, people respond by telling me their memories about their mother's or grandmother's pressure cooker. Most have a horror story to tell.

So, let me tell you about my mother's pressure cooker. Whenever Mom used her cooker I stayed away from the kitchen. The loud hissing noises and the rocking and shaking of the jiggler on top scared me. And the time that the food was blown all over the kitchen convinced me that I NEVER wanted one of those. But about 20 years later, I heard about the "new" pressure cookers and decided to give one a try. And even though I was interested, it still took a couple of years after my intention to actually get up the courage to buy one. Many of my students let their cookers languish in the box for months, but once they try it, there's no going back.

Now I have been using a pressure cooker for almost a decade. I consider it one of my most essential pieces of kitchen equipment. I've even packed and hauled it for car camping trips. It's fast, uses less fuel or energy and best of all, it makes food taste great. You get that satisfying next-day taste of soups, stew and chili right away. You save money by cooking dry beans instead of buying them in cans. It's easy to eat more whole grains, since they cook in less than half the time of cooking on the stovetop. Fast cooking makes time spent in the kitchen more enjoyable. I can decide what to eat and have it on the table in an hour or less. Once you try pressure cooking, you might be hooked. As for explosions, those are only related to taste.

Garlicky Green Bean Potato Salad

Makes 8 cups
3 minutes high pressure; then quick release.

Y ou can substitute wax or purple beans for the green beans in this recipe. The key to having it turn out is to be sure that the potatoes are cooked and the green beans are not overcooked which is why you put the beans on top of the potatoes. This may be my favorite summer potato salad, and I have many.

1 1/2   **pounds potatoes, like Yellow Finn or Yukon Gold**
1/2   **pound green, yellow or purple beans**
8-10   **cloves garlic, peeled**
3/4   **cup vegetable broth**
2   **tablespoons rice vinegar**
2   **tablespoons extra virgin olive oil**
2   **teaspoons Dijon mustard**
2   **tablespoons vegetable broth**
1   **clove garlic, crushed (optional)**
Salt and pepper, to taste

Cut potatoes in half lengthwise, and again in half so you have quarters. Then slice into 1/2-inch thick pieces. Snap stems off beans, and cut into 2-inch segments.

Add vegetable broth to cooker. Lay potato pieces on the bottom. Insert garlic cloves between the potato slices. Place the green beans on top. Lock the lid in place. Turn heat to high. Once the cooker comes to high pressure, reduce heat to low.

Maintain high pressure for 3 minutes. Release pressure with a quick release method. Remove potatoes and green beans to a large bowl to cool slightly.

Put cooked garlic into a blender with the remaining dressing ingredients. Process until dressing is creamy. Pour over potato-green bean mixture. Taste, adding salt and pepper, if necessary. Serve warm or chill. If chilled, stir before serving.

How a Pressure Cooker Works

Boiling water on the stove top takes place at 212°F. Once you lock the lid on the pressure cooker and it comes up to 15 pounds p.s.i. (per square inch) the temperature inside the cooker climbs to over 250 degrees, resulting in hot steam. This process makes the food cook much more quickly, causing the flavors to get infused into the food.

I like the "new" pressure cookers that have a spring valve instead of a jiggler. Usually they are stainless steel pots with triple-ply bottoms that work well, even as a large pot for stove top cooking. These cookers usually have at least four pressure release valves, so the lid is unlikely to blow off. If you have an older style, jiggler cooker and like it, then continue using it carefully.

The basic technique for using the cooker is to either add all the ingredients, lock the lid on and bring the contents to a boil over high heat to get to pressure, or to first sauté ingredients, add some liquid and then turn the heat up high. Once pressure is achieved, set your timer, lower the heat to maintain pressure and wait for the timer to beep. You will then either quick release the pressure (which is a major improvement in the "new" cookers) at the stove or run it under cold water. Or, if the recipe calls for it, you will use a natural pressure release, which takes from 5 to 10 minutes, depending on how much food is in the pot. Be aware that the food is still cooking during the natural pressure release. Always remove the lid, tilting it away from you to avoid getting burned by the steam.

You do need to be careful when cooking foods with a naturally high sugar content, such as leeks, tomatoes and other tomato products, as they are more likely to stick to the bottom of the cooker and burn.

Do not walk away from your pressure cooker or leave the house, as my friend Carol did. The cooker did not explode, but it took lots of elbow grease to get it clean again. It's best to stay near your pot and prevent burning.

If you should ever forget about your cooker and need to clean it, I recommend filling it with water, a lot of baking soda and bringing that to a boil. Turn off the heat and let it sit for an hour or so, and then scrub with stainless steel, steel wool or similar abrasive until your pot is clean again.

If this isn't enough information for you, be sure to look for any books by Lorna Sass on pressure cooking. She has great recipes and has been my pressure cooking inspiration and mentor.

Orange Scented Beet Salad

Makes 4 1-cup servings of beets plus 1/2 cup greens
3 minutes high pressure; 7 minutes natural pressure release

*C*ooking beets has never been easier. They become so tender you don't even
need to peel them.

1 1/2 pounds beets, about 6 medium
1/2   cup freshly squeezed orange juice
2   tablespoons cider vinegar
3   3-inch long pieces of orange peel, using only the colored part of the peel
2   tablespoons Sucanat or brown sugar
2   teaspoons Dijon mustard
2   teaspoons orange zest
2   green onions, sliced
2   cups spicy greens like arugula, mustard or a mix, washed and dried

Scrub beets. Remove tops, stems and tails and cut in half. Then cut into
1/4-inch slices.

Put the orange juice, vinegar and the large slices of orange zest into the
cooker. Add the beet slices. Lock on the lid. Bring the pressure to high over
high heat. Reduce the heat to maintain high pressure for 3 minutes. Remove
the pot from the heat. Let the pressure come down naturally for 7 minutes,
then release any remaining pressure.

Remove the lid, tilting it away from you. Remove the large pieces of
orange zest. Stir in the brown sugar and mustard.

Remove the beets from the cooking liquid and let cool for 5 minutes. Mix
the 2 teaspoons orange zest and green onions with the beets. Pour the liquid
from the cooker over the beets. Spoon 1/4 of the mixture onto 1/2 cup of
spicy greens on individual salad plates. Or you may chill the beets, without
the zest and green onions, and let sit in the liquid for a day or two. Right
before serving stir in the orange zest and green onions.

"Some more beets ma'am, please"

That was the message from my friend Cathy on my answering machine one day. Cathy agreed to be a recipe taster the day before and obviously she liked what I made, Orange Scented Beet Salad on Spicy Greens.

The color of beets scares many people. They are just so red. Well, that issue can be resolved by using gold or white beets, if you can get them. Chioggia beets are pinkish with concentric circles of white inside and aren't quite as messy as the red ones. I don't like to cook with red beets because they color everything they come in contact with, even one's hands. And when I'm teaching cooking, flesh-colored hands look best.

Beets are incredibly sweet and delicious. Pair them with something a bit acidic such as citrus juice or vinegar to provide flavor contrast.

Also, when you buy beets you get two vegetables - the root and the greens. Immediately remove the greens from the beets and put them in a separate bag. The beets breathe through the greens, so both the roots and greens will stay fresher if they are separated.

A fantastic thing about beets is that they are available for many months during the year, though they are sweetest in the winter which is the best time to roast them. Roasting beets or any other root vegetable accentuates their natural sweetness.

Roasting beets makes it easy to make one of those fancy beet salads that cost six dollars and up at restaurants. You know the kind, with slices of beets, greens, some crumbled cheese and toasted nuts. You can easily replicate this type of salad at home. To roast a beet, put it whole or cut in half or more, depending upon its size, in a glass baking dish. Add a few tablespoons of water to the dish. Cover the dish and put in a 400 degree F. oven for 30 minutes to 1 hour, or until a knife is easily inserted. Let it cool and peel off the skin. Use in any way that you'd like including slicing into cubes, rounds or irregular chunks.

There is a mistaken impression that because of their bright color, beets are incredibly good for you. Truth is that they are high in Vitamin A and contain a decent amount of iron, Vitamin C and fiber, but aren't one of the nutrition powerhouses like kale or sweet potatoes. But that's no reason not to eat them. It may turn out that they contain an important phytochemical that's yet to be discovered. Try them, they can't be beat.

Three Grain Summer Vegetable Salad

Makes 4 servings
5 minutes at high pressure, 7 minutes natural pressure release

*T*his fiber-filled salad is easy to prepare, since the three grains cook together. It is colorful and delicious. I developed this recipe for Cooking Light magazine, which is where it first appeared.

Vegetable cooking spray
1/4   cup minced onion
1   cup white basmati rice
1/2   cup millet
1/2   cup quinoa, rinsed and drained
2   cups water
1   cup apple juice
1   cinnamon stick
3   green onions, diced
1   medium apple, cored and diced
1/3   cup raisins
1/2   cup chopped red or yellow pepper
1/4   cup chopped cilantro
2   teaspoons curry powder
1/2   teaspoon salt
4   tablespoons nonfat or lite mayonnaise
2   tablespoons lemon juice
1/2   teaspoon salt

Spray the cooker with vegetable spray. Add the onion and sauté over medium heat for 1 to 2 minutes. Add the grains and toast for 30 seconds. Add the water, juice and cinnamon stick. Stir once. Lock on the lid. Bring to high pressure over high heat. Reduce the heat to low and maintain high pressure for 5 minutes.

Remove pot from the heat. Let the pressure come down naturally for 7 minutes. Release any remaining pressure. Remove the lid, tilting it away from you. Remove the cinnamon stick. Fluff the grains with a fork. Put into a large bowl and let cool for 5 minutes.

When the grains have cooled, mix in the green onions, apple, raisins, pepper, cilantro, curry powder and salt. Then stir in the mayonnaise, lemon juice and salt. Serve at room temperature or chilled.

Basic Risotto

Serves 4-6
5 minutes high pressure; quick release

*R*isotto is delicious and EASY in the pressure cooker. If the risotto is not creamy enough when you open the lid, then add more liquid. If the risotto is too runny, then cook it on the stovetop for a few minutes until it reaches the consistency that you like.

1   tablespoon oil
1 1/2 - 2 cups sliced leek, about 1-2 medium leeks, white part only or onion
1 1/2 cups arborio rice
1/2   cup dry white wine
3 1/2 - 4 1/2 cups homemade vegetable stock or water and chicken-flavored broth powder
1/2   teaspoon lemon zest
2   teaspoons white balsamic vinegar
1/2   teaspoon salt
Freshly ground pepper, to taste
Grated cheese (optional)

Heat the oil in the cooker over medium heat. Add the leeks and cook for 2 minutes. Add the rice, stirring to coat with the oil for about 1 minute. Add the wine, standing back to avoid sputtering oil. Stir well. Then add 3 1/2 cups of the stock. Stir well.

Lock the lid in place. Over high heat, bring the cooker to high pressure. Reduce the heat to low to maintain high pressure. Cook at high pressure for 5 minutes. Reduce the pressure with a quick release. Remove the lid, tilting it away from you.

Add the lemon zest and balsamic vinegar. Taste and add salt and pepper. Serve immediately in shallow soup bowls. Pass the cheese on the side, if desired.

Risotto variations: Only long cooking vegetables such as mushrooms, potatoes or winter squash should be added at the beginning of the cooking process, since most vegetables will overcook in 5 minutes. The rice is usually so hot that you can just stir in your favorite raw vegetables at the end. If they need to cook longer give them a few minutes cooking on top of the stove. Some of my favorite combinations are spinach with grated nutmeg and lemon; green beans and tomatoes; winter squash and greens such as kale; peas and asparagus. The possibilities seem endless.

Simple Vegetable Stock

Makes 8 cups
5 minutes at high pressure; natural pressure release

*I*t's great to have homemade stock. When I double the recipe, I freeze half in zippered bags, freezer containers or ice cube trays. The stock cubes are great when you just need a couple of tablespoons for a recipe. I prefer not to salt my stock, adding salt to taste when using it in cooking. Do remember to do this, as unsalted stock is bland compared to canned stock. Use stock anywhere that you would use broth.

4-6	cups assorted vegetable scraps, saved over time in your freezer or the equivalent of fresh vegetables
2	medium onions, peeled and quartered
2	cups leek leaves
3-4	garlic cloves (optional)
3	carrots, cut into chunks
3	ribs (stalks) celery, cut into pieces
2	bay leaves
A few peppercorns	
2	sprigs thyme or savory, or other herbs of your choosing (beware of using rosemary as it can be overpowering)
10	cups pure water

Put all the ingredients in the pressure cooker (frozen vegetable scraps do not need to be thawed). Lock the lid in place. Bring to high pressure over high heat. Lower the heat to maintain high pressure. When five minutes is up, turn off the heat and let the pressure come down naturally.

Remove the lid, tilting it away from you.

Allow the stock to cool slightly. Then pour the stock through a strainer into containers (not directly into zippered bags). When you get to the vegetable matter, press it against the strainer to extract all the liquid and flavor. Cool and refrigerate for a few days, or keep in the freezer for up to 3 months.

Taking Stock of Stock

Sometimes it seems so much easier to grab the aseptic box off the store shelf and put it in my pantry than to take the time to make stock. My remedy for the reluctance I feel about making stock is to save suitable vegetable scraps and put them in a plastic bag in the refrigerator or freezer so they are ready when inspiration strikes. Some situations make it easy to keep stock making in mind.

In the winter my husband Rick has carrots and celery in his lunch so I save all the ends and pieces daily. I also save onion scraps, green onion and leek leaves, garlic nubs, celery root, winter squash, Jerusalem artichoke and potato peelings in my bag.

You can make your stock to complement your soup. Save asparagus and mushroom stems separately because their flavors can be overpowering. I use ginger for an Asian flair. For Allium Broth (see page 52), use only members of the onion family. Broth can be simple, using only asparagus ends, green garlic and a few herbs in the spring. In the summer I make sweet corn stock with the cobs left after removing the kernels.

Usually I add to the stockpot a Mediterranean (not California) bay leaf or two, some peppercorns, and a few sprigs of fresh cut herbs, such as thyme or savory. What stays out of the pot are any cruciferous vegetables, as their taste is concentrated when cooked and becomes overpowering. Avoid adding any of the following: cabbage, cauliflower, broccoli, Brussels sprouts, kohlrabi, kale, rutabaga, turnips or their greens.

If you like a richer-flavored stock, you can take whole cut-up ingredients like those in this stock recipe (rather than scraps), coat them with a tablespoon of oil and put them on a baking sheet into a 450 degree F. oven for about 30 minutes. The roasted vegetables caramelize, adding flavor depth and sweetness. Use the caramelized veggies as the basis for your stock. Add water and continue with the recipe.

Stock possibilities are endless and healthy without all the sodium found in boxed or canned stock or broth. My stock reflects the flavors I seek. Let yours do the same.

Shane's Fabulous Lentil Soup

Makes about 8 cups
6 minutes high pressure; 10 minutes natural pressure release

*M*y son Shane's favorite dinner used to be my lentil soup. He brought this soup to his kindergarten class for a project that he did on lentils and all the kids enjoyed it. It is easy to make, extremely nutritious and keeps well in the freezer for up to 4 months.

1	onion, chopped
2	carrots, chopped
2	bay leaves
2	sprigs fresh thyme and/or savory
6	cups water or broth
1 1/2	cups green or brown lentils
1/2	cup red lentils
1	medium potato, diced (does not have to be peeled, just scrubbed)
2	teaspoons Organic Gourmet Vegetable Seasoning paste or 1 teaspoon salt

Freshly ground black pepper, to taste

Put the cooker over medium heat. Add the onion and dry sauté for about 2 minutes, adding a tablespoon of the water if sticking occurs. Add the carrots and sauté for another minute. Add the bay leaves, thyme or savory (or both), water, both types of lentils, potato and Vegetable Seasoning paste (if using salt add after lentils are cooked). Stir well. Lock the lid in place on the cooker and bring the mixture to a boil over high heat until you achieve high pressure. Then reduce the heat to maintain pressure for 6 minutes. Remove from the heat and let the pressure come down naturally. Remove the lid, tilting it away from you. Remove the bay leaves and add pepper to taste. If using salt in lieu of Vegetable Seasoning paste, add it now.

Note: *You may add 1 cup corn after removing the pressure cooker lid. Remember that this soup is hotter than any soup made on the stove, so let it cool accordingly, or add an ice cube to each bowl, if necessary.*

White Bean and Escarole Soup with Sage

Makes 8 1-cup servings
7 minutes high pressure, 10 minutes natural pressure release

*T*his soup tastes so fresh and the colors are attractive. If you have two or three medium tomatoes on hand, chop and add them after you release the pressure. Just give them a good stir. Escarole looks like lettuce but it's bitter. It mellows when cooked.

2	cups Cannellini (Italian white kidney) or Great Northern beans, presoaked or quick soaked (see page 17)
1	medium onion, diced to equal 1 cup
2	cloves garlic,
1	cup diced potatoes
6	cups vegetable broth
2	bay leaves
4	sprigs of sage, plus some for garnish
2	cloves garlic, minced
1	head of escarole, chopped to equal 4 cups
1	tablespoon lemon juice or white balsamic vinegar

Salt and pepper, to taste

Put the cooker over medium heat. Add the onion and sauté for 2 minutes. Add the whole garlic cloves and sauté 1 minute more.

Add the beans, potatoes, broth, bay leaves and sage. Lock on the lid. Turn heat to high and bring to high pressure. Set timer for 7 minutes, and then turn heat down to low to maintain high pressure.

After 7 minutes, when the timer sounds, turn off heat and move pot to a cool spot on the stove. Let the pressure come down naturally for 10 minutes, then release any remaining pressure.

Remove the lid carefully, tilting it away from you. Remove the bay leaves and sage sprigs. Using a hand blender, mix the hot soup until it is mostly creamy, with a few whole beans left in for texture. Add the remaining sage, minced garlic and chopped escarole.

Put the pot back on the heat and stir, cooking for 2 to 3 minutes until the escarole is wilted and cooked through. Taste, add lemon juice or vinegar and adjust seasonings. Serve hot.

Potato Leek Soup

Makes 8 cups
4 minutes at high pressure; quick release

I like my potato leek soup really creamy, blending it thoroughly. If you like yours chunkier, then don't blend it as much. If you like thinner soup, add water or broth until it's the desired consistency. McDougallers can just omit the oil and watch for sticking leeks. You don't have to worry about sputtering oil.

1	tablespoon olive or canola oil
3	large leeks, washed well, sliced lengthwise and cut into 1/2-inch slices
4	large russet or Yukon gold potatoes, peeled and cut into 2-inch pieces
3	tablespoons chicken flavored or veggie broth powder
6	cups water
1	tablespoon chopped fresh thyme or 2 tablespoons dried thyme
2	bay leaves
1	teaspoon salt, or to taste

Chopped Italian parsley or chive flowers, for garnish

Add the oil to the cooker over medium heat. Sauté the leeks for about 3 minutes, adding water if they begin to stick. Add the potatoes, broth powder, boiling water, thyme, bay leaves and salt, standing back to avoid sputtering oil. Lock the lid in place and bring to high pressure over high heat. Reduce the heat to maintain high pressure and cook for 4 minutes.

Reduce the pressure with a quick release method. Remove the lid, tilting it away from you, to allow any excess steam to escape.

Remove the bay leaves. Puree the soup with a hand blender until it is the desired consistency, or remove some of the potato mixture and puree carefully in a blender or food processor. (This can be done in the blender by filling the container half full or less, covering the top of the container with plastic wrap, putting the lid on and covering that with a towel.)

Taste the soup once blended, adding salt if necessary. Garnish with chopped Italian parsley or chive flowers, if you have them.

Three Sisters Stew

5 minutes high pressure; natural release

*T*he basis of Native American cooking is corn, beans and squash. I like to throw in tomatoes and chiles or red bell peppers to round out the dish, if they are in season. This stew is best in October or November when winter squash and corn are both fresh.

1   cup Anasazi, red or kidney beans,
      soaked overnight or quick soaked
1   tablespoon canola oil
1   large onion, chopped
1   chipotle chile, seeded, cut into pieces
1   teaspoon cumin seeds
2   teaspoons dried oregano
1 1/4 cups boiling water
1   pound organic delicata, kabocha or butternut squash,
      seeded and cut into 1-inch chunks
      (if organic, does not necessarily need to be peeled)
10   sundried tomatoes, cut into pieces
1   medium red pepper, cut into strips and then diced
1   tablespoon fresh sage, chopped or 1 teaspoon dried sage
1   cup corn, cut from the cob, or frozen, thawed
1   Anaheim or Poblano chili, roasted and diced
Tamari to taste
1/2   cup green onions, sliced
1/4   cup toasted pumpkin seeds, for garnish

Heat the canola oil in the cooker over medium heat. Add the onion and sauté for 2 minutes. Add the chipotle chili, cumin seeds and oregano and cook for 1 minute. Then add the drained beans, boiling water, squash, sundried tomatoes, red pepper and sage. Lock the lid in place. Bring to high pressure over high heat. Reduce the heat to low and maintain high pressure for 5 minutes.

Let the pressure come down naturally. Remove the lid, tilting it away from you. Stir in the corn, roasted pepper, tamari and green onions. Cook for a minute or two to be sure that corn is cooked through.

Serve hot, garnishing with toasted pumpkin seeds.

Garlic Parsley Mashed Potatoes

Serves 4 - 6
4 minutes at high pressure; quick release

*C*ooking potatoes this way means that making real mashed potatoes takes just minutes. Make them as lumpy or smooth as you like.

4   medium russet, yellow Finn or
      Yukon Gold potatoes
1   cup vegetable broth or
      water and chicken flavored broth powder
6   cloves garlic, peeled and cut in half
1/2   cup soy milk or other milk
Salt
1/4   cup chopped parsley

Cut each potato into 8 to 12 chunks. Put into the cooker with the broth and the garlic. Cook for 4 minutes at high pressure. Release the pressure, carefully removing the lid. Mash the potatoes with a masher or a hand blender. Depending upon the consistency you want, add all the soy milk or not. Add salt to taste and parsley and stir to combine. Serve hot.

How to Choose a Cooker and What to Put in It

For me, size is the biggest determining factor in choosing a cooker. No matter which brand of pressure cooker you choose, remember that the pot can only be filled one-half to two thirds full, depending upon the contents. I suggest choosing the largest cooker, 6-quart or more, that your budget and cabinetry will allow.

The two brands of cookers that I like best are from Spain. Fagor makes a number of spring valve models, from 4-quart to 10-quart. Their newest design the UCook is the most versatile and includes both 4- and 6-quart pots that stack one inside the other for storage, and with a lid that can be used on either pot. It comes with two steamer baskets that sit above the bottom of the pot, allowing you to cook 2 different dishes at once, and a glass lid so you can use the spare pot for stovetop cooking.

Fagor also has a modified jiggle-top model that I only recommend if you liked your mother's pressure cooker.

My other favorite brand of cooker is Magefesa. The Super Rapid II was great, yet it is unfortunately no longer available in this country and has been replaced by the Classic model. The only reason that I cannot recommend it is that I have not used it.

I suspect that other brands of cookers are equally as functional. Look for stainless steel pots with thick bottoms, with easy closing lids and quick pressure release features. These cookers will cost between $70 and $150, and you can often buy them on sale. If you find one for far less, you may want to thoroughly investigate what it can and cannot do.

No matter which cooker you buy, I always suggest that you start using it by putting in plain water and bringing it to pressure so that you can feel comfortable with it and how it reacts to heat and pressure. It will help prevent the potential of ruining food on your first try.

Most cookers require 1/4 to 1/2 cup water or other liquid to help them get to pressure. Be sure to follow the manufacturer's recommendations. Watery foods sometimes contribute their liquid to the amount you add, so keep that in mind. Generally the best dishes to prepare in a pressure cooker are soups, stews, chili, beans and grains. I also have a technique for Braised Tofu and Vegetables (see page 120), which is one of the quickest and tastiest dishes that I make.

You need to be watchful and use a timer when making quick-cooking vegetables. A 30-second difference when cooking broccoli or asparagus means the difference between having a crisp, bright green vegetable and one that is mushy and gray. That's why many people reserve their vegetable cooking to artichokes. But I promise that your cooker can do much more for you.

I fell in love with my cooker when I started making Shane's Fabulous Lentil Soup (see page 113). I felt like the best mother in the world when Shane was little, because I could make him tasty soup from scratch in less than 10 minutes. But it took so long to cool, I always had to remember to add an ice cube.

Be glad, especially during hot summer weather, that the pressure cooker may change your cooking life. You don't have to stand the heat of the kitchen for nearly as long as before.

Smoky Sweet Potato and Black Bean Chili

8 minutes at high pressure; natural pressure release; 5 minutes stovetop cooking
Serves 6 to 8

*I*nspired by a recipe in Simple Vegetarian Pleasures by Jeanne Lemlin, the sweet potatoes provide an interesting taste and texture to this chili. The smokiness of the chipotle pepper adds a special dimension and flavor. If corn is in season, you can add it at the end of cooking.

1	tablespoon canola oil
2	large onions, finely diced
6	garlic cloves, minced
2	red bell peppers, chopped
2	tablespoons chile powder
2	teaspoons ground cumin
1	teaspoon dried oregano
1/2	teaspoon chipotle chile powder or 1 chipotle chili, chopped, seeds removed
2	medium sweet potatoes yams, peeled and cut into 1/2-inch dice
2	cups black beans, presoaked
1 1/2	cups water
3	cups finely chopped tomatoes, fresh or canned
1/4	cup tomato paste
1/2	teaspoon salt

Chopped cilantro for garnish

Heat the oil in the cooker over medium heat. Add the onions and cook for 3 minutes. Add the garlic, red peppers and spices and cook another 2 minutes. Add the yams, black beans and water. Lock the lid in place and bring to high pressure over high heat. Reduce the heat to low to maintain high pressure.

After 8 minutes, remove from the heat and let the pressure come down naturally, which takes about 10 minutes.

When the pressure is down, remove the lid tilting it away from you. Add the tomatoes and tomato paste and salt. Cook over medium heat for about 5 minutes, until the tomatoes have broken down into a sauce. Remove the whole chipotle pepper if you used it. Taste and adjust seasonings. Serve over rice, or other grain, garnished with cilantro.

Chickpeas Italiano

12 minutes high pressure; natural pressure release; 5 minutes stovetop cooking

*C*hickpeas (garbanzos) are one of my favorite beans and here they get the Italian treatment. It's important to cook the beans before adding the tomatoes, or else they won't cook through and remain tough. I always recommend a quick-soak for beans (see page 17).

11/2 cups chickpeas (garbanzo beans), presoaked
1 tablespoon olive oil
2 medium onions, diced
3 cloves garlic, chopped
1 1/2 cups vegetable broth
3 tablespoons chopped basil
2 teaspoons fresh oregano or
  1 tablespoon dried oregano leaves
1 bay leaf
2 cups chopped fresh or canned tomatoes
1 tablespoon extra virgin olive oil
1 clove garlic, minced
2 tablespoons Italian parsley, chopped
2 tablespoons basil, chopped
1 tablespoon balsamic vinegar
Salt and pepper

Heat the olive oil in the cooker over medium heat. Sauté the onion for 3 minutes. Add the garlic and sauté another minute. Add the beans, broth, 3 tablespoons chopped basil, oregano and bay leaf. Bring to high pressure over high heat. Lower heat to maintain high pressure and cook for 12 minutes. Let the pressure come down naturally.

Remove the lid, tilting it away from you. (Taste the beans to be sure that they are cooked to your desired consistency. If not, put them back on the heat for another couple of minutes at high pressure, and then let the pressure come down naturally again.) Remove the bay leaf and add the tomatoes. Cook over medium heat for 5 minutes, until the tomatoes break down. Remove 1 cup of the bean mixture and puree in a food processor or blender. Return to the pot with the olive oil, garlic, parsley and basil. Stir in the vinegar and then add salt and pepper to taste.

Braised Tofu and Vegetables

Serves 4
2 minutes high pressure; quick release, stove top cooking if necessary

*T*his is a simple and tasty way to prepare tofu and vegetables. Pressure cooking changes the texture of tofu so that everyone likes it.

1	tablespoon oil
1	pound firm tofu, drained and cut into cubes
2	onions, coarsely chopped
3	cloves garlic, minced
1	teaspoon finely minced ginger
2	carrots, cut into 1-inch sections on the diagonal
2	ribs celery, cut into 1-inch sections on the diagonal
1/4	cup vegetable stock
2	tablespoons tamari or soy sauce
1	teaspoon sesame oil
1	tablespoon water
2	teaspoons arrowroot powder

Heat the oil in the cooker over medium heat. Add the tofu cubes, onion, garlic and ginger and sauté for 2-3 minutes. If anything starts sticking, add some stock and scrape the pot to remove the stuck-on parts. Add the carrots, celery and 2 tablespoons of the stock and cook another minute or so. Add the remaining stock and the tamari. Bring to high pressure over high heat. After 2 minutes release the pressure. Stir in the sesame oil. If the sauce seems too runny, combine the water and arrowroot and stir into the pot. Add more tamari to taste. Serve hot over rice, quinoa or noodles.

Note: *You can use other vegetables in this recipe such as broccoli. cauliflower, asparagus or peas, being careful not to let them overcook. Put them on top of the other ingredients to slow down the cooking.*

Pressure Cooking Basics

Always follow the manufacturer's directions regarding the minimum amount of liquid to add to your cooker.

Never fill your cooker more than one-half to two-thirds full, depending upon what you are cooking.

When adapting traditional recipes to the pressure cooker, usually you will need to add more herbs and spices and less liquid.

Decrease the cooking time compared to standard recipes by 75 percent and see how things turn out. It is easy to get the pot back up to high pressure and continue cooking, but once you have overcooked certain foods they are not especially appealing. Follow the charts in Lorna Sass' *Great Vegetarian Cooking Under Pressure*.

Be careful when sautéing ingredients containing natural sugars such as onions, leeks, shallots, carrots and tomatoes. Anything that sticks to the bottom of the cooker will burn when the heat is turned on the high setting to bring the cooker up to pressure. To prevent burning, add some water or other liquid and give a good stir on the bottom of the pot to loosen any stuck-on bits of food.

Remember to set your timer when the cooker reaches desired pressure and turn the heat down to maintain that pressure setting. Do not walk away, take a shower or leave the kitchen or the house until the pressure has come down and the heat is no longer on.

Upon opening the cooker, tilt the lid away from you so that the extremely hot steam does not burn you.

Remember that food coming out of the cooker will be hotter than food cooked by other methods, so warn people before they eat it.

Enjoy using your cooker and spend your "extra time" reading a book, smelling the flowers or thinking about your next quick and tasty meal.

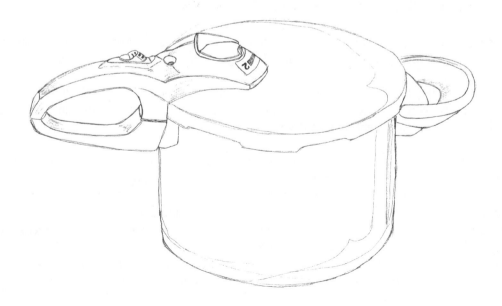

Glossary of Food Items

This brief list will help you use some of the recipes in this book.

Agar agar – a seaweed gelatin that is used for its gelling properties. It must be cooked to be effective. It comes in powder, flakes or bars. I usually use the powder and buy it in bulk. The price per pound is high, yet a little goes a long way. One teaspoon of powder will usually gel a pint of liquid.

Agave syrup – this sweetener is a better alternative than honey for sweetening. It is a bit sweeter than brown rice or barley malt syrup but has a low glycemic index (GI). You can always use it instead of Sucanat or sugar in salad dressings or other liquid applications.

Arrowroot – a starch from a root used in place of cornstarch, which is processed. Use it by mixing with liquid and stirring well. You can add it directly to the ingredients in hot pots or pans, but works best when the pan is removed from direct heat as the arrowroot tends to clump. Purchase in bulk for best price.

Bragg's liquid amino acids – use in the same way as tamari or soy sauce, in equal amounts. It is salty. Contains amino acids and is not fermented.

Chicken flavored broth powder – there isn't any chicken in here, so don't worry. I use this to "beef" up the flavor of soups. If I have any of my own stock, I use it instead of the broth powder and water combination. The powder is usually sold in bulk in natural food stores or you can buy it in bottles from Rapunzel.

Egg replacer – a powder made from starches that can be mixed with water to replace eggs in recipes. Purchase at natural food stores in bulk, bags or boxes. The most common brand is Ener-G.

Escarole – a type of endive that looks like a dark-leaf lettuce but it is bitter. When cooked the flavor mellows. If you love bitter tastes, you can eat it raw.

Gomashio or gomasio – a combination of salt and sesame seeds or salt, seaweed and sesame seeds good for sprinkling on foods. I like the Eden brand. Sea vegetables add important minerals to our diet.

Kaffir lime leaves – I buy these frozen at my local Asian foods store. You can grow Kaffir lime trees here in California and other warm climates. If you can't find them, substitute ? teaspoon grated lime zest and a couple teaspoons lime juice to replicate the flavor.

Lemon olive oil – this is an infused oil used for flavoring, not cooking. This type of oil varies widely in price and taste. My favorite is organic Meyer lemon oil. A few drops go a long way.

Lemongrass – the stalk of a lemongrass plant. You can grow it outdoors or in a pot, or find it in Asian groceries, natural food stores and some supermarkets. When using it, remove some of the outer stalk. Then bruise the stalk by carefully hitting it with the blunt part of your knife. Cut into 1-inch or larger pieces. Be sure to remove these after cooking, as they are woody and tough. You can use dried lemongrass if that is what you have. Otherwise, use a bit of grated lemon zest to replicate the flavor.

The Veggie Queen™

Miso - fermented soybean paste, which is very salty. There are many types and brands of miso, and the flavor of each differs. In my refrigerator you'll find Mellow White Miso, which is mild and good for salad dressings and dips, and then a stronger type such as barley or red miso for soups and stews (but do not boil it, add after high heat cooking is completed). Try a few kinds to decide which you like. Miso lasts for a year or more in the refrigerator. Use it sparingly or it can overpower your food. Westbrae is a commonly available brand, although South River miso is extremely delicious and more delicate.

Nori – seaweed or sea vegetable that is made into sheets, and used for making rolled sushi. It comes toasted and untoasted. You can toast the untoasted type by holding it over a flame for a few minutes.

Nutritional yeast – a yellow powder or flake that is a seasoning and dietary supplement (B vitamins). It has a nutty, cheesy taste and is easily added to gravies, salad dressings or sauces. It is not brewer's or baking yeast. Purchase it in bulk at natural food stores and store in the refrigerator.

Rice paper wrappers – dried, thin sheets or rounds, made from rice flour and water, sold in Asian groceries, natural food stores and some supermarkets. They come in a variety of sizes and shapes. I prefer the 6-inch diameter rounds.

Seitan – also known as wheat gluten. It is chewy and can be used to replace meat in recipes. It does not have much flavor. You can buy a boxed mix and make it yourself or buy it already prepared in cartons with marinade, or frozen. Purchase at natural food or Asian stores.

Silken Tofu – made by Mori Nu. It comes in an aseptic box that is currently 12.3 ounces. It is shelf-stable and good for a year from when it is made, and does not need refrigeration until after it is opened. Once you open the box, cover with water and change the water daily to keep your tofu fresh for up to 1 week. I use this type of tofu only for blending in sauces, soups and dressings, not for stir-fries or baked tofu. It comes in soft, firm and extra-firm. I find the latter two interchangeable. You can substitute the silken tofu that comes refrigerated in water if you must.

Sucanat - natural sugar cane juice. It is unrefined and substitutes one to one for sugar, although the color is darker. Use sparingly, as you would sugar.

Stevia – a plant sweetener that is 10 to 100 times sweeter than sugar, depending upon its form – pure powder, mixed powder or liquid. While not specifically called for in this book's recipes, you can use it in place of sugar, especially in salad dressings and stir fry sauces. A few drops are all you need to substitute for a teaspoon of Sucanat or sugar. The taste can be overpowering, so use it sparingly.

Tahini – raw or roasted sesame seed paste. I prefer raw but buy what you can find in jars or cans at the natural food store, supermarket or Middle Eastern grocery. You can make your own tahini, which is essentially what I do in Sweetheart of a Salad (page 71). The two tablespoons ground seeds in that recipe is equivalent to one tablespoon of tahini.

Tamari – a dark, wheat-free, sauce made from fermented soybeans. The flavor is much better than standard soy sauce, which is mostly salt, water and coloring. Japanese shoyu is a good substitute. I use San-J reduced sodium tamari since it is available at most natural food stores.

Tempeh - a fermented soybean cake with origins from Indonesia, where they have used it for 5000 years. It is less processed than tofu and has a nutty taste and firm texture. You can buy it in natural food stores and some supermarkets. Often it is frozen. Do not eat tempeh without cooking it. Steaming it first helps it absorb flavors.

TVP – textured vegetable protein that is processed, extruded soy. I use the small granules in Herbed Lentil Burgers (page 99). It can also easily be added to tomato sauce or chili. I purchase it in bulk but it also comes in packages. I don't use this often. You can substitute frozen, thawed and crumbled tofu.

Ume plum vinegar - not a true vinegar, but leftover from the process of pickling ume (small, Japanese plums). It is salty and pink and can be used anytime that you would use vinegar and salt. The flavor is difficult to describe. A little goes a long way. Eden is my favorite brand.

Wasabi powder – a spicy green powder that is mixed with water to form a paste, traditionally served alongside sushi.

Vegetable cooking spray – this usually refers to a spray oil product such as Pam®. I prefer putting the oil of my choice, usuallly grapeseed, avocado, canola, olive or a combination of them, in a spray bottle such as Misto®. Most commercial sprays contain lecithin, which burns at a lower temperature than oil and can make your cookware permanently sticky.

Zest – the outer, colored part of the peel on citrus fruit. Use any but grapefruit since it is too bitter. Zest has anti-cancer properties and adds flavor bursts without any fat. Avoid the white pith under the peel, as it can be bitter. Use only organic fruit when zesting. The best way to do this is with a tool called a zester or a Microplane™ grater.

For more thorough ingredient explanations, I suggest that you purchase or review The New Whole Foods Encyclopedia by Rebecca Wood, Penguin, 1999.

Sources

If you don't live near a major city, you might find it easier to get some ingredients by mail order or online. This isn't all-inclusive but will give you a good start.

Alter Eco™ – they carry fair-trade certified and organic products from around the world that include ruby rice, purple rice, regular and red quinoa. They are sold in boxes but worth paying for packaging to support people with integrity, both the farmers and the company.
www.altereco-usa.com

Bob's Red Mill – a larger, independently owned natural food products company that carries whole grains, beans, spices, baking ingredients and many gluten-free items. They are moving more into organics and their products are easy to get in stores and online.
www.bobsredmill.com

Cook's Garden – if you're a gardener, find great vegetable seeds, along with recipes and information from Ellen Ogden, who knows lots about vegetables.
www.cooksgarden.com or call 1-800-457-9703

Earthy Delights – carries a variety of dried and fresh mushrooms plus some wild foods.
http://www.earthy.com/index.cfm or 1- 800-367-4709

Goldmine Trading – carries many natural and organic products, as well as a complete line of macrobiotic products.
www.goldminenaturalfood.com or 1-800-475-FOOD

Gourmet Mushrooms – local to my area, they offer a variety of fresh and dried mushrooms, growing kits and medicinal mushroom products.
www.gmushrooms.com or 1-800- 789-9121

Indian Harvest – carries a variety of heirloom beans and whole grains.
www.indianharvest.com or call 1-800-346-7032

Lotus Foods – sells gourmet rice from around the world including the red rice in one of the recipes plus black, brown and white rice. You'll also find red and black rice flour under the rice and grains category at www.worldpantry.com or call 1-866-972-6879. These and other grains available at www.farawayfoods.com.

Melissa's- all kinds of produce and other ingredients to peruse.
www.melissas.com or call 1-800-588-0151

Oh! Tommy Boy's – Organic potato farm located in Petaluma, California. Heidi Kirkland who co-owns it with her husband Tom plans to sell seed potatoes. You'll be able to grow your own.
www.farmtrails.org/ohtommyboys

Rancho Gordo – some of the best heirloom beans that you can get with many varieties available. They also have quinoa, posole and some dried herbs available.
www.ranchogordo.com

Tierra Vegetables – Known for their chipotle chiles, chile powder and chile jam, they also grow fresh produce and have other products. They are right here in Santa Rosa, California, my hometown.
www.tierravegetables.com or call 1-888-7TIERRA

Index

C

Cabbage
  Asian Slaw 94
  Cabbage and Red Apple Slaw 72
  Chinese "No-Chicken" Salad 94
  Sautéed Red Cabbage 53
Cannellini or Great Northern beans
  Fasoulia 16
  White Bean and Escarole Soup with Sage 114
Capers
  Eggplant "Caviar" 20
  Grilled Ratatouille 33
  Roasted Red Pepper Relish 42
Cardamom, ground
  Fruited Wild Rice 57
Carrot(s)
  Carrots with Honey, Lime and Dill 8
  Diced Onions, Parsnips, Carrots and Apple with Sweet
  and Spicy Sauce 53
  Seasonal Sweet and Sour Veggie Stir-Fry 102
Casserole
  Layered Polenta Casserole 81
  Shepherd's Pie 80
Cauliflower
  Red Rice Salad with Lemony Roasted Cauliflower 73
Celery Root (celeriac)
  Herb Roasted Root Vegetables 54
Cereal flakes
  "Unstuffy" Stuffing with Mushrooms and Walnuts 56
Cheese, Nondairy – soy, rice, almond or other
  Beet, Potato and Leek Gratin 78
  Layered Polenta Casserole 81
  Potato and Kohlrabi Gratin 58
  Spinach, Leek and Mushroom Quiche with an Oat Crust 79
Chickpeas, see Garbanzo beans
Chile Pepper, see Pepper, Chile
Chili
  Smoky Sweet Potato and Black Bean Chili 118
Chili paste with Garlic
  Spicy Citrus Sauce 88
  Szechuan Eggplant Roll-Ups 39
Chili powder
  Roasted Vegetable Fajitas 34
Chilled Soup see Soup, chilled
Chipotle pepper
  Hot and Smoky Potato Salad with Chipotle Peppers 48
  Smoky Gazpacho 32
  Smoky Sweet Potato and Black Bean Chili 118
  Three Sisters Stew 116
Chives
  Mediterranean French Green Lentils 17
  Orange and Onion Salad on Greens 2
Chutney
  Fresh Fruit Chutney 40
Cilantro
  Andean Corn and Quinoa Salad 28
  Asian Slaw 94
  Chinese "No-Chicken" Salad 94
  Floribbean Summer Fruit Salsa Salad 23
  Fresh Fruit Chutney 40
  Hot and Smoky Potato Salad with Chipotle Peppers 48
  Smoky Gazpacho 32
  Thai-inspired Broccoli Slaw 47
  Thai Rice, Snow Pea and Mushroom Salad 4
  Three Grain Summer Vegetable Salad 110

Coconut milk
  Thai-inspired Broccoli Slaw 47
  Thai Rice, Snow Pea and Mushroom Salad 4
Cold soup, see Soup, chilled
Collard Greens
  Greens Braised with Tomatoes and Thyme 55
Cooking spray, see Vegetable cooking spray
Coriander, seeds
  Grilled Ratatouille 33
Corn
  Andean Corn and Quinoa Salad 28
  Pasta with Tempeh-Corn Sauce 35
  Three Sisters Stew 116
  Tomatillo, Summer Vegetable, Brown and Wild Rice
  Salad 25
Cornmeal, see polenta
Cranberries, fresh or dried
  Bright Autumn Salad 46
  Cranberry Orange Relish 43
  Fruited Wild Rice 57
  Jerusalem Artichoke Salad with Arugula and Cranberry
  Vinaigrette 70
  Pear and Toasted Walnut Salad with Cranberry
  Vinaigrette 45
Cucumber
  Chilled Cucumber Dill Soup 32
  Floribbean Summer Fruit Salsa Salad 23
  Oriental Cucumber Salad 3
  Smoky Gazpacho 32
Currants
  Mediterranean French Green Lentils 17
  Fruited Wild Rice 57
  Stuffed Swiss Chard 62
Curry
  Curried Lentils and Rice 101
  Curried Pear and Squash Soup 75
  Curried White and Sweet Potato with Fresh Fruit
  Chutney 40
  Three Grain Summer Vegetable Salad 110

D

Daikon, see also radish
  Rice and Veggie Sushi Salad 92
Dates
  Spiced Sweet Potato Pie 65
Delicata squash
  Curried Pear and Squash Soup 75
Desserts
  Spiced Sweet Potato Pie 65
  Squash custard 64
Dill
  Carrots with Honey, Lime and Dill 8
  Chilled Cucumber Dill Soup 32
Dips
  Eggplant "Caviar" 20
  Lemon Scented Spinach Spread 41
Dressings
  Caesary Salad Dressing 91
  Creamy Roasted Red Pepper Dressing 90
  Oil Substitute for Salad Dressing 93
  Warm Sesame Dressing 72
  Zesty Lemon Garlic Dressing 91
Dried Beans, see specific types
Dried fruit
  Fruited Wild Rice 57

Vegetables Get The Royal Treatment

Harvest Time?

I don't recall exactly when I first met Larry Tristano of Triple T Ranch and Farm but he attended the downtown Santa Rosa market on weeknights at least 8 years ago. His stall was located away from the other farmers so it got my attention as I'm always on the lookout for great produce.

Shortly thereafter, Larry showed up at the Santa Rosa Saturday farmer's market that I attend much of the year. As I do with most of the farmers, we started talking. Usually it's about the produce they are selling, yet Larry, his son Vince and son-in-law, also Larry, shared more.

I learned that they were hunters. Larry, the elder, told me that he harvests elk and other animals. He feels that if the population were not kept under control there would be problems. We've had many discussions about hunting since then.

Do I care that Larry is a hunter? Morally, I do. Yet, Larry is extremely generous, donating his beautiful, organically grown produce and eggs for events and photo shoots. His salad mix, peppers, squash, greens and other vegetables are grown right here in Santa Rosa. Larry's heart seems to be in the right place despite his gun practices. (A friend told me that Larry cheerfully delivered fresh produce to her without a delivery charge when she was homebound and unable to get to the farmer's market. Imagine a farmer making house calls!) Larry and I may never see eye to eye about hunting but I'm on the hunt for great produce and it speaks for itself.

Besides, Larry always winks and invites me to feel his face when he's clean-shaven. Occasionally he gives me a hug. That's the true difference between shopping at the supermarket and the farmer's market. I hope that you'll get to meet farmers like Larry, perhaps without the guns.

More of What They're Saying about The Veggie Queen

What a great cookbook. Jill Nussinow is dedicated to both the health of incorporating veggies into your diet, and the passion for making truly delicious food. I love food and love to cook, and I found some new ideas here - The Veggie Queen had some new ways of working with healthy but sometimes puzzling ingredients like nutritional yeast, and after reading this book, I'm going to pull out my pressure cooker (a gift I've never used), and armed with her book, I'm looking forward to trying some 20-minute (or less) healthy soups and stews. — Annie B. Kay, MS, RD, RYT, Author of *Every Bite Is Divine*

Everything about this book rates 5 stars. The cover and the graphics are lovely but the academy award goes to the recipes. I cannot imagine anyone reading this book and not wanting to eat more than 5 (veggies) a day. Jill, a registered dietitian: an expert, has managed to make a great deal of in-depth information clear and interesting. I will be making many of the recipes in this book, for Thanksgiving and all through the year and plan to give this book as a gift to many of my veg challenged friends. Yum, thanks Jill. — Fran Costigan, author of *More Great, Good Dairy-Free Desserts*

Between the cover and the index is where the real glory is held, in the recipes. The book is not too thick and not too thin, a welcome change from the sea of fat cookbooks that are squeezed onto my cookbook shelf with only a few useful recipes inside. With the Veggie Queen's support, I am eager to visit the farmer's market and fill my plate with five to nine servings of vegetables a day! — April Sullivan, *Reader Views*, www.readerviews.com

Jill Nussinow teaches the reader to prepare vegetables in a wide variety of scrumptious ways, from Smoky Gazpacho to Roasted Red Pepper and Tomato Soup to Winter Squash Enchiladas and much more. All recipes are delineated with extensive, crystal-clear step-by-step instructions. A mouth-watering way to enrich one's diet with healthy vegetable dishes. No vegetarian cookbook collection would be complete without the inclusion of The Veggie Queen! — *Midwest Book Review*

Perhaps my favorite part of this book is The Veggie Queen's Morsels and Tidbits sprinkled throughout. After reading this cookbook (which I did from cover to cover), I not only had some terrific ideas for vegetables, including ones I rarely eat or have never tried, I also felt that I knew the author. These short essays based on childhood memories, conversations with friends and fun experiences like growing mushrooms in the bathtub are witty, informative, and above all, fun to read. — Melanie Wilson, www.vegetarianbaby.com

It's surprising that so many vegetarian cookbooks feature a paucity of vegetables. But not "The Veggie Queen"! Here, we have one sumptuous recipe after another, each loaded with a variety of delicious veggies. This is the ultimate cookbook for upgrading your diet to include the freshest vegetables from every season. — Erik Marcus, Author of *Meat Market: Animals, Ethics and Money*, Publisher of Vegan.com

I've read a lot of boring vegetarian cookbooks. This is not one of them. Jill's recipes taste delicious twice: first in your mind and then in your mouth. — Nan Kathryn Fuchs, PhD, Editor, *Women's Health Letter*

"Jill's seasonal recipes give us cause to celebrate what's ripe." — Lorna Sass, author of *Lorna Sass Whole Grains Every Day, Every Way*."

If you are passionate, or just curious, about vegetables, then the Veggie Queen™ has a book for you. A great resource on what to do with all the veggies you collect at the market — from picking and storing them to cooking with them. This book will appeal to both beginning chef and gourmand alike with its enticing, well thought out recipes." — Eric Tucker, chef and cookbook author, *The Artful Vegan and The Millennium Cookbook*

Vegetables do really get the royal treatment in Jill Nussinow?s book. She has a deep respect for seasonality and a very broad range of recipes. And Jill really knows how to put some depth into vegan cooking. — Martha Rose Shulman, author of *Mediterranean Light and Ready When You Are*

QUICK ORDER FORM

If you enjoyed this book and would like to give a copy to someone else, you may obtain one at your favorite bookstore, online bookseller or use a copy of the form below.

Phone: 1-800-9191-VEG (834), toll-free. Have your credit card handy.

Email: www.vegetarianconnection.com or jill@vegetarianconnection.com

Mail: PO Box 6042, Santa Rosa, CA 95406-0042

Shipping: $5.00 for first item, $2.50 for each additional item

Sales tax: For shipping in California, please add 8% sales tax

Also available:

Book and Pressure Cooking DVD together for $36.95 plus shipping of $7.00

Name: _____

Address: _____

City/ State: _____   Zip: _____

Telephone: _____

Email: _____

Payment::

❒ Check   ❒ Visa   ❒ Mastercard

Card Number: _____

Name on card: _____   Expiration date: _____